NOTES TO MY CHILDREN

— A Simplified Metaphysics

KEN CAREY *is a*

wonderful expression of the Creator.

To Brad & Jo

Aloha,

Mel

Dec. 1986

Cover Art: Reginald Birch
Illustration Page *vi*:   Doug and Wilma Jordan
Other Illustrations: Colleen Haarbrucker and Aurora

Other books by Ken Carey:

The Starseed Transmissions

*Terra Christa: The Global
Spiritual Awakening*

NOTES TO MY CHILDREN

— A Simplified Metaphysics

Introduction

Chapter 1. . . . . . The Empire Of The Sun (Part One). 1

The Empire Of The Sun (Part Two) 9

The Empire Of The Sun (Part Three) 19

Chapter 2. . . . . . Playing Since The Beginning Of Time 25

Chapter 3. . . . . . Dressed Up In Matter. 33

Chapter 4. . . . . . You Are The One Things Come To. 39

Chapter 5. . . . . . The Wishing Tree. 49

Chapter 6. . . . . . Some Of Us May Remember. 59

Chapter 7. . . . . . A Wave Of Awakening 65

Chapter 8. . . . . . Christmas Morning For The Family Of Man. 73

Chapter 9. . . . . . I Am The River 81

Chapter 10. . . . . A Family Of God Beings. 89

Chapter 11. . . . . Starlight, Stardust. 95

Chapter 12. . . . . Tracking God In An Enchanted Land 101

Chapter 13. . . . . Mirrors and Magic 109

Chapter 14. . . . . Child Spirit. 119

Chapter 15. . . . . Elves and Jumping Mice 125

Chapter 16. . . . . The Harvest — One World Ends, Another Begins. 135

Chapter 17. . . . . The Lord's Prayer. 143

Chapter 18. . . . . The Shepherd's Psalm (Part One) 151

The Shepherd's Psalm (Part Two) 161

INTRODUCTION

I have always felt that upon incarnation, upon becoming conscious in a physical body, our children were due some kind of report — something that would let them know what kind of planet they had surfaced on, what the conditions were in this particular age, what the basic game plan was and what strategies they might realistically adopt. This book is based on talks that I had with my own children attempting to provide them with precisely this information. My parables are not meant to be taken literally; they are designed to awaken and nourish the child spirit in all. To that unencumbered spirit I dedicate this book — let the particulars fall where they may.

Ken Carey

Spring 1982

Chapter 1

THE EMPIRE OF THE SUN

(Part One)

Do you like to draw pictures? God likes to draw pictures. Once upon a time God drew some three-dimensional pictures that people could walk in. With a brush made of sunlight, God carefully touched the Earth and painted wonderful landscapes, beautiful valleys and hills and mountains and rivers and seashores and oceans and lakes and deserts and pastures and fields — deep, dark forests. With the brush of sunlight, God painted wonderful things on the surface of this world.

When God finished painting beautiful forests and fields and streams and rivers, He took His magic brush and began to paint all kinds of animals. These animals could actually walk and talk because when God paints things with a brush of sunlight, they are painted in a much better way than any person could paint them with a brush of paint on a piece of paper. When God painted these animals, they actually ran through the forests and fields. Sometimes He would dip His brush of sunlight in a certain kind of earth. Sometimes He would dip it in clay. Sometimes He would dip it in the sea. Then He would paint.

When God painted the animals, He dipped His brush in the grasses and in things that were already growing. He painted all kinds of wonderful animals. The animals lived

in the pictures that God had painted and had made come to life.

One day God thought it would be good to have some people in the pictures, some people to walk on the land and to sit on the grass in the meadow under the trees on still afternoons. God wanted people who could enjoy and appreciate all the things that He had painted on the world with His magic brush. He wanted to be inside of the pictures that He had painted. So God got ready to begin painting people. He dipped His brush in all the things that had been already painted. He dipped His brush of sunlight in the ocean and in the animal kingdom and in the vegetables and plants and flowers and trees and forests. He dipped it in the mountains and volcanoes so the people would have some fire in their blood. He dipped it in the rivers and the deserts, in the ice and snow, and in the hot winds. He dipped it in the rain. When it was ready, He painted the first people. He painted people with His brush of sunlight and they lived in a land called the "Empire of the Sun" in the middle of a peace-filled sea.

Pacific means peace-filled. In the middle of the peace-filled sea God had painted the most beautiful of all the lands that He had painted on Earth. It was a magical country of mountains and deserts and hills and streams and rivers and fishes and flowers and birds — incredible birds, birds with all kinds of colored feathers, big birds that could walk. There were even horses and animals that could talk. God painted the first people in the middle of this wonderful land and God breathed the breath of life into them and they came alive. The land was called the Empire of the Sun because the people lived in the starlight from this nearest star and the starlight lived in the people. The consciousness of God filled the people's hearts.

Now the reason God created people was to sing the songs of God in the lands that He had made. He created them to play their magic flutes to the trees and to the flowers and to the animals that He had made. People would sing the songs of God, the songs of the seasons, the songs that would make the springtime come, songs that would make the summer come with its fruit and watermelon, songs that would make the fall come with its bright colors, songs that would make gentle frosts come and turn the leaves sparkling gold and silver. There wasn't much snow in the land (in the higher places on the mountains there was a bit), but there were wonderful sparkling frosts that used to come in the winter, beautiful icicles which would cover the trees at higher altitudes. Mostly it was a warm land, the Empire of the Sun, and the people were filled with the Sun as the Sun lived in people and people lived in the Sun.

It was a wonderful land and a special time. A beautiful and seemingly endless age when wonderful and magical creation took place. The people were good. They were centered in God and they loved the beautiful pictures that God had made. They sang songs to the mountains and to the lakes. They sang songs to the trees and to the hills. They used to say that the wind that blew through their land was the whispering of the Sun. And it was true. The Sun was whispering magical words of love to the Earth as the wind blew across the face of the land. As the sacred words were whispered things blossomed and grew. People sang songs in the wind and the wind blew through the people as it blew through the trees. The spirit of God that made these pictures in the land of the Empire of the Sun was alive and well and healthy. God walked with the people and talked with the people and told the people wonderful stories and helped them in their days. Because the people walked with God and talked with God, the people also talked with the animals. The animals talked back. Each animal spoke in a strange kind of song that the people of that day could understand. They would sing back the same kind of songs to the animals. The animals understood and were their friends. In those days the animals loved the people, all the animals, even the lions and tigers. The animals weren't wild then. They loved the people and were happy to do whatever the people wanted. They would do anything to please the people.

God made this land, the Empire of the Sun, in the middle of the peace-filled sea, a land of rich scents and beautiful smells, a land of colorful vistas and beautiful views. There were sparkling still lakes, lakes high in the mountains so still that they reflected the stars at night perfectly. You could sit at the edge of one of those lakes on a silent night and you could look into the still water and count the stars. One particular lake was so still you could even see the reflection of the milky way in its midnight waters.

Other things were still in that land as well. The people's hearts were still. They weren't filled with troubled feelings and worried thoughts. God made wonderful sounds in that land and the people could hear God. They could hear the songs that God wanted to sing through them. The people were the instruments on which God played His favorite music. Some of the people would sing of the trees. Deep in the woods God would sing through them His forest song. God would tell things to the trees in the music that He played through the people who walked in the forest in those days.

With other people God would go to the mountains and sing sacred songs to the mountains telling of His love. God lives in the middle of the Sun and, remember, this was the Empire of the Sun. The Sun whispered wonderful things to the Earth and sang wonderful songs through the people who walked on the Earth and let the Sun live in their hearts. In the Empire of the Sun the people let the starlight shine from their eyes. There were beautiful things to smell and to see and to hear and to touch, sparkling cool waters to swim in. In the day you would swim in those still lakes and the water was just the right temperature to be wonderfully refreshing. The rivers were sweet, so fresh and clear you could drink out of them. There was nothing in those days to make the rivers dirty or impure because the people didn't think that anything could be impure. The people's hearts were pure, still and quiet like the lakes always were when nobody was swimming in them.

All the land was full of wonderful things to see: snow-capped mountains, rivers, hills, trees, jungle forests, oceans, waves splashing against the beach. There were wonderful things to hear; music that God would sing through the people. There were wonderful things to smell; flowers and roses. There were things to touch and places to swim. The food was plentiful and delicous, mostly fruit, many kinds of fruit, some of which still exist in the Hawaiian Islands. The Hawaiian Islands are the only part of the Empire of the Sun, except for Japan and a few smaller islands here and there, that are still above water. But we'll get to that part of the story in a minute.

The food was so plentiful and nourishing in the Empire of the Sun that the people didn't have to work. They didn't have tractors in those days. They didn't plant seeds and they didn't eat heavy dense food. The fruit was light and filled with the radiance of the Sun. Because the people knew how to talk to the plants, the plants did whatever the people wanted and cooperated in wonderful ways. The plants couldn't talk in the same way that the animals could. The trees would whisper things when the wind blew through them. The people asked the trees to produce things that looked like the Sun. "We want

something to eat that is like the Sun," they said, "because we love the Sun so much as it shines in the heavens above us, we want to eat it. Of course we know we can't eat it because it's fire and it's hot and besides if we ate it, it wouldn't be there anymore to shine on us and to bring up all the wonderful things out of the Earth. But maybe you could make something for us to eat which would look bright like the Sun and would taste like light." So, the trees did.

The land was filled with things that were infinitely pleasing to all the senses. The fruits of the land were abundant. All the things that God painted with the brush of the Sun on the paper of the lands that floated on the peace-filled sea filled up the senses of the people. Their senses were filled and they lived in joy. The Sun lived in them and they lived in the Sun as ages and ages wandered by. Then do you remember what happened? I think we can all remember something about this. It was us after all. The reason people don't remember what happened is because they don't want to think about it. They don't want to think about it because it makes them too sad to think about how they blew it. Let's just keep telling it as if it were a story that happened to other people. Some of us might remember, but we can still talk about it as if it were a story. But before we start to talk about the trouble, before we mention the bad things that started to happen, I want to tell you something else.

THE EMPIRE OF THE SUN

(Part Two)

All that God made filled up the senses of the people. The people's senses were full with rich fragrances and tastes and things to feel and see. Music was continually echoing throughout the hills and the valleys and the forests. The children of the Sun were filled with life. Their senses were overflowing. They used their senses in a way that people today have forgotten. They didn't just take things in with their eyes, they gave out light with their eyes. They could walk in the darkness. They could see in the dark even if there were clouds in front of the stars and no moon.

When it was silent and still, people could still hear. Their ears would hear the music of their souls. God sang them into being and they always heard their song. They were singing for God and speaking for God. They used the sound of their voices to make a joyful noise, a happy song, a song of celebration. All their days were thankful. They had everything that anyone could ever dream of. God had created all things for them. God had painted them with the brush of starlight. Everything was perfect and fine and beautiful. People in those times used their senses to fill up creation with the richness and the wonder of their love.

They sang their songs in the villages. Their eyes

painted colors on everything they saw. The towns were happy places where people gathered together to make songs of many instruments and voices, places where they could share things in a way that they couldn't when they were walking by themselves along the seashore or in the forest. God, you remember, walked with the people in those days. The people let God live in their hearts. In the evening they would walk together. And they shared many things, many ideas and many plans. The people were thankful for all that God had made in the Empire of the Sun.

One day the people said, "God, can we help you paint with the brush of the Sun? It looks like you have so much fun when you paint with the rays of starlight from this closest star. We watched you the other day painting those animals that we call giraffes. We watched you paint sheep too. It was really interesting to see how you used the brush of starlight to paint those animals and then how you breathed the breath of life and whispered to them and how they came alive and began to dance. They are so cuddly and soft. We thought it would be fun if we could help you do that, if we could paint some things too. Would you let us use your brush of starlight? Would you let us use your brush of starlight so we could paint this picture too? Maybe we could paint new trees. Maybe we could even paint rivers and forests."

In those days, the land that lay in the middle of the peace-filled sea was a land of flowing things. Changes came more rapidly there than in the world as we know it today. God could paint with the brush of the Sun and a river would bubble up in one day. God could look at a spot like this and say "It would be nice to let there be a spring here." He would take the brush of the Sun, paint a spring, and a spring of sparkling crystal clear blue water would come bubbling up out of the Earth and begin flowing downhill. When the people asked God if they could help, God said, "Sure. That would be fun. You can help me paint some pictures in this land too. You could paint your own pictures and then live inside. Together we could paint wonderful things. You probably have some good ideas.

"OK, I'll teach you how to use the brush of starlight. I'll teach you how to paint animals. I'll teach you how to paint trees. And I'll teach you how to paint mountains and rivers and all the things that you want to paint. But you must remember one thing. It's very important. Listen carefully. This is something you have to remember if you're going to use these brushes of starlight to create things. Whatever you create must be something which will make everybody happy, not just something which will make you happy, all by yourself. It has to be something for the good of the whole. It has to be something which will make all the people in this land happy. If you remember that always I'll show you how to use the brush of the Sun."

So, there in the Empire of the Sun, in the middle of the peace-filled sea, many thousands of years ago, God taught the people how to paint with the brush of the Sun. He taught people to take the light that came from each star, a special kind of rainbow, a spectrum of magical colors, and using the special ray that would come from each star the people at night, when the stars shone, painted delicate things that could fly through the air on tiny wings. Insects, people call them today, but in those days people called them fairies. They became insects after people began to make some mistakes. In the beginning they were called fairies, little things that flew through the air, each painted by a single ray of starlight with the spectrum of a starlight rainbow on its wings. During the day the people learned to paint with the brush of the Sun.

They painted forests on the land, great forests with trees much bigger than any we see today. They let them grow longer. You might have a tree as big around as a small room with the next closest tree many yards away. Because the trees were farther apart the brush would always grow thick underneath the trees. So one day the people took the brush of the Sun and painted an animal to eat the brush down. Can you guess what animal? Goats. They painted goats with the brush of the Sun and they let the goats eat the brush of the Earth so they could walk in the forests. There was lots of space underneath the big trees after that. You could walk for days and days without leaving the shelter of the forest.

One day the squirrels told the people that it was all right with them if they made the trees far apart. They knew this would give the people room for the parties that they liked to have at night in the starlight under the trees. But the squirrels asked the people if they would please space the trees so their edges were touching. The squirrels wanted to be able to run from treetop to treetop. This is the quickest way for a squirrel to get around. Now, in those days, in the western part of the Empire of the Sun, there was a great forest that covered that whole part of the land. A squirrel could run from treetop to treetop all the way from the north Pacific sea to the south Pacific sea, from the northern coast to the southern coast without ever touching the ground. It took the squirrels a long time to do this, but they weren't in any hurry.

Nobody was in a hurry in those days. The people took their time because they didn't know about some things. If we met some of those people today, we might think they were kind of dumb. There were lots of things they didn't know about. You know one of the things they didn't have any idea about? Tomorrow. They didn't even have a word for tomorrow. They didn't know what such a

thing was. They didn't have a word for yesterday. You see they didn't need to plant seeds or anything. They didn't have to plan like we have to plan now. When they wanted to eat, they would just ask the trees to grow magical fruits for them.

Sometimes, the trees grew fruit which looked like the Sun because the people loved the Sun so much they wanted to eat it. Sometimes the trees grew fruit which looked like little trees because people loved the trees so much they wanted to eat them, but of course they couldn't. Often, the trees grew fruit that represented the essences of a particular river or a particular stream or a mountain that was special to them. Before the Fall the people never wanted a thing. They didn't know what desire was. They didn't know what wanting was. They lived the moments of their days in the Empire of the Sun filled with a spirit of peace and thankfulness, appreciating everything that was around them. They painted all kinds of wonderful things with the brush of the Sun. Today there are still remnants here and there of the things that we painted originally when we lived in the Empire of the Sun, although many of these things have changed since we have changed.

People never created other people. That was one of the rules that God made. It had to be for the good of the whole. People could only paint lower forms of life than themselves. They couldn't paint themselves. It would be like somebody trying to look at his own eye without a mirror. But people could paint any kind of animal they could imagine. There were unicorns in those days, beautiful white unicorns like horses but with a single horn in the middle of their foreheads. People also painted dragons, but the dragons weren't wicked. The dragons were special creatures that flew through the air. Dragons were very smart. They were the part of the animal kingdom that

told the people the most about the other animals. Dragons were the smartest animal and knew more about the animal kingdom than any of the other animals.

But anyway, let me tell you what happened. One of God's rules was that people had to take care of whatever they painted with the brush of the Sun. They couldn't paint a finch, say, and then not take care of it, just turn around and forget it. They couldn't paint an animal that needed certain things to take care of it without also making sure that they painted a picture around that animal in which the animal would be happy. In other words, if they wanted to paint a certain kind of creature, they had to also paint a picture around that creature that made it easy and comfortable for the creature to live. Whatever they made they were responsible for. And sometimes it took a while to paint things with the brush of the Sun. Sometimes it wasn't all done in one day.

One evening there was a lady who was painting something with the brush of the Sun. It was something very special, something very exciting, one of the neatest things that anybody had thought of. She got a little too excited as she was painting it because she saw all the wonderful things that it could do and she did something that wasn't for the good of the whole. She did something that seemed right to her, but she knew that it wasn't the best thing for everybody. Soon her friend came along. His name was Adam. She told Adam what she had done and Adam said, "Whoa, wait a minute. When God told us we could use these brushes of starlight and sunlight, He said that we had to be careful not to ever paint anything that wasn't for the good of the whole." Then Eve — for this was none other than Eve herself — turned to Adam and said, "But this is for the good of most of the whole. Really it is. See, look here. See how good it is for this part of the whole?"

"Yeah, well, I guess it is good for this part of the whole," Adam replied, "but it isn't good for the whole." Eve looked up and smiled. "But it won't hurt the whole. I don't see how it could possibly hurt the rest of the whole, do you? There is nothing evil about it." "Well, you've already done it," Adam said. "You've got to take care of it now. It's too late, you've already made it. How are you ever going to take care of it?" "I don't know," Eve said. "I really don't know." Then Eve began to cry and Adam agreed to help her.

Now the creature Eve was painting was an animal, a very smart animal, an animal with a hungry earthbound way of looking at things. It might have been all right if Adam and Eve had worked with God in painting this thing and allowed it to be completed so that it was for the good of the whole. I don't want to dwell on this part of the story. I'll just say for now that something was done that wasn't supposed to be done. Soon other people became interested in Eve's project. It seemed like it might be for the good of some of the whole at least. Soon other people said, "Hey, look, we can do some things here too. It doesn't seem all that wrong." Nothing bad happened right away. But God had told them that if they didn't think of the whole when they painted with the brush of the Sun, they would surely die.

The people weren't sure what death meant, though they suspected it was something bad. After they broke God's law they didn't die right away. Everything kept going on, it seemed as usual. Other people came around. They were interested in what Eve had created. They saw Adam helping her now. So these other people started painting things with their brushes of the Sun too, things that seemed good to them. They didn't bother to check with God.

Before long, most of the people in the Empire of the

Sun were using the creative power of God to create things that seemed good to them, but weren't really for the good of the whole. They lost their connection with God. The Sun didn't shine as brightly after that. More and more clouds began to cover the land. Fog started drifting up from the valleys at night, thicker than before. The days became more and more overcast as time went on. Pretty soon the storms grew louder and wilder. People weren't always able to get things to go the way they wanted them to anymore because a lot of other people were creating things that they thought were good. Sometimes what one person thought was a good thing wasn't what somebody else thought was a good thing. Soon these things started bumping into each other. By now the weather was getting wild. And as there were more conflicts among the people, tornadoes and hurricanes began to trouble the villages. There never used to be these kinds of things before. Storms became violent. There was more thunder and lightning; soon volcanoes were erupting and shooting off big steams. Even the Earth began to tremble.

THE EMPIRE OF THE SUN

(Part Three)

As the Earth trembled people started to get scared. A group of us said, "Hey, we gotta get back talking to God again." Now God had already walked around in the Empire of the Sun several different times looking for His people. "Please, where are you?" He would say. "Where are you?" But the people were all hiding. God tried to tell them, "Hey look, this is silly. You don't realize what you are doing. I know you think it's fun to create these things without checking with me, but these things are going to destroy you. You are creating monsters. You're creating things that are going to come back and hurt you." But the people didn't listen. They saw God coming and they knew they had done something bad.

The people all went and hid. This was silly. They could have just said, "We're sorry. We shouldn't have done that, God. We won't do it anymore. Tell us how we can fix it up." And God would have said "Sure." They could have fixed it up in no time and everything could have been wonderful again. But they hid from God and five times God walked through the land and said, "Where are you people? Where are you?" Soon, because they spent so much time hiding in the shadows, the people lost their bodies of light.

In those days people had bodies made mostly of

starlight with just a small percentage of physical substance. Their bodies had physical substance in them but they were mostly made of the Sun. The largest part of them was of the Sun.

When they began creating all these mixed-up things, they created vibrations that made the still lake rough and choppy. And you know when a lake gets full of ripples, it doesn't reflect things. Now they would go down to the beach at night and they couldn't see stars in the lake anymore. One of their favorite things to do was to go down to the beach at night, walk out on the pier, and look at the stars reflected in the lake. But now the lake was always ripply because the winds were no longer gentle. The winds were getting violent. The people's hearts were churning. They lost their bodies of light and became naked.

Before the people started creating things that weren't for the best of the whole, they saw the Earth through the eyes of the Sun. Their bodies were of the Sun and they were sons and daughters of God. They were children of God walking in the land that God had made, beginning to paint the picture that they lived in with God. When the trouble came, like I was telling you, the winds began to get wild, the fog drifted up from the valleys at night, the weather became overcast, volcanoes began to go off, earthquakes began to rumble and the land began to shake violently. Soon a whole part of the beautiful Empire of the Sun fell into the sea. There was still a big part left but the whole western part fell into the sea. That is when this group of us got together. Some of us right here in the circle.

We said, "Hey, remember God came walking around in the garden just a little while ago and we hid in the bushes? Look, He's going to come around again in the cool of the day. I know He is. This time let's be out there waiting for Him. Did you see what happened to all that land that sunk into the ocean? See the clouds, feel the weather and the winds, feel the Earth rumble? We've really messed this thing up. This land is like a delicate engine that is running way too fast and wild. The whole continent is trembling and shaking. It is way out of balance."

So a few people met with God then. They knew that they were without their bodies of light, but God forgave them and clothed them again in new bodies of light. He talked to them about a time when they would return to the Earth to help bring the Kingdom of the Sun back into the world again. But these were just a few. Most of the people were afraid to talk to God. They started getting in boats to leave the land. They knew that the rest of the land would sink soon. They could feel the volcanoes rumbling and the Earth shaking. They got into boats and they left Lemuria, which is another name for the Empire of the Sun, and they took boats to South America and China. They took boats to Australia, the Phillipines, and India. Some of them sailed to Africa. All over the world the people set up villages that they thought would be like the Empire of the Sun.

God saw them as they left for all these lands. And He saw that they were naked. They had lost their bodies of light. They had no way to experience sensation, no way to touch, no way to taste anything, no way to feel anything, all because they had not listened to God. But God knew that there was a way for them to come back again into the light. God knew that there was a way for them to move once more with His spirit. So God made skins for them, animal skins. He clothed them in the skins that we have today. These skins that we have today are the skins that God sewed for people as they left the Empire of the Sun.

Finally, except for Hawaii and Japan and a few islands in the South Pacific, the Empire of the Sun disappeared

into the sea. The sea was again filled with peace, untroubled by the distortions that selfish human beings had
brought into the Earth. By sinking the original Empire of
the Sun, what we sometimes call the "Motherland", God
had taken away the worst people who were doing the
worst things. They all disappeared, bubbling under the
waves. This was the lowest point to which people fell. In
some places people forgot about the Motherland and
turned into cavemen. In Mexico, Egypt, and Ireland they
built civilizations based on what they remembered of
their lost home. Languages changed. The tower of Babel
took place. People's skins became different in the various
lands they settled. They began to think differently. They
began to fight and quarrel.

People's bodies today are made up of more substance of
Earth and not as much substance of the Sun. People have
come to reflect their environment instead of making the
environment reflect their spirit. This is all backwards.
People are supposed to be the representatives of the Sun.
It is through the sunlight and starlight shining out
through our lives that the environment is supposed to be
dressed and kept in spirit. When God dressed us up in
these bodies that we have today, He told us that for our
sakes we would have to work until who we think we are is
once again returned to the ground of being, to the ground
of being that made all the things of the Earth, to the God
who painted all the pictures on the Earth. Until that happens, we will have to have certain kinds of relationships
with one another that will teach us what we forgot.

As we find ourselves waking up and remembering this
story today, I want to tell you some wonderful news. The
Empire of the Sun still fills the heavens around the
Earth. God's thought are still here. God's songs are
still here for people to hear, but we have to listen. We
have to listen to the voice of God as He walks in the gar-

den in the cool of the day. It's the cool evening of the day right now and God is singing His song, creating each of us in His image and likeness in the Empire of the Sun. When we allow our hearts to be still, when we allow our emotions to be untroubled, we can reflect God's ideas. We can begin to see the Empire of the Sun here right now. We begin to see all the beautiful things that are around us. We don't see the shadows so often anymore. Sometimes we recognize them and we welcome them into our awareness. But the shadows disappear in the light that shines from our eyes when we see the Sun in everything.

Today we live in the Sun and the Sun lives in us. God the Father, the Creator of this whole beautiful world, the Creator of this garden, the Creator of Eden, is here again because we're here. God can see with our eyes and hear with our ears. God can taste with our lips and speak with our voices. He can feel with our hands and smell with our senses. Because we see with the eyes of the Sun, we see what's behind all these things. We see the Empire of the Sun, the Kingdom of Heaven behind all things, behind all forms. As we see the Empire of the Sun, we help to bring it back.

Chapter 2

PLAYING SINCE THE BEGINNING OF TIME

Have you ever been surfing? Have you ever gone for a ride on the big waves on the surface of the ocean? There are different ways to do it. You can ride them on an air mattress. You can ride them on a surfboard. You can even go body surfing all by yourself. You stand out a ways and wait for a big wave to come. Then you dive in front of it. It quickly pushes you along. You feel like an arrow might feel when it is shot from a bow. If you miss, you get all tangled and twisted up. A surfboard is a long narrow board like a big double ski. You take it with you to a good spot in the ocean and wait for a big wave. Then you stand on this board and ride it in. It's really fun.

Suppose you were a little creature that lived at the bottom of the ocean where the water is always cold and dark and still. You might not even know that there was any such thing as a wave. At the bottom of the ocean it's cold and still. The further away you go from the surface where there is light and fresh air, the colder and stiller it gets. The deeper you go, the more pressure there is. It pushes in your ears.

Imagine that all your life you have lived on the bottom of the ocean in the dark, still water. One day you discover the waves on top and learn how to surf. You go back down to the bottom of the ocean and you say to your friends, "Hey, listen to this, you won't believe it. There are huge waves up there!" And everybody says, "What are waves? What are you talking about? I've never seen a wave. I'm

an old crab, I've never seen a wave." Your friends don't want to believe that there are any such thing as waves because they've never seen them, they've never had any experience of them — the water at the bottom is still. You not only saw the waves, you actually learned how to surf. You had a wonderful and glorious time. So you went back down to the bottom where all your friends were living. You told them all how fun it is up there on the surface. You talked about the fresh air and the sunshine and the waves to your friends, but they didn't have any words for waves. They had always stayed deep in the water. They had never experienced that kind of movement. They didn't have any way to say wave. You wanted to explain it to them, so you had to think up stories to sort of tell them about what it is like. As people of the Earth, we do this too. We use children's stories, fairy tales, myths and legends to explain something of which the world of Earth people have little experience.

There are waves in the world that people live in. There are great cosmic waves of energy that move through this world all the time, tremendous wonderful waves of energy. People don't experience them or feel them because they are out of alignment. Suppose you have a radio set and you are about to turn to your favorite station. But before you can, your mother or father or somebody changes it to another station that has the news on. Well, both stations are still there in that same room. You know that the station you want to hear is right there, but you have to tune the radio differently to pick up the music, the rhythm, the harmony that you really want to hear. You may not be particularly interested in the news.

This is what it's like right here. There is something perfectly delightful happening all around us every moment, all the time, something more wonderful than you could ever imagine. But we are like receivers that aren't tuned to pick it up. Everybody in the world is tuned the wrong way. The dial is loose and keeps drifting back and forth. Sometimes people pick up one station, sometimes another. Just when you start to get into one station, it drifts over and picks up another. People don't stay focused. There are always these random thoughts coming in. When they come people identify with them and think that they are their thoughts. One minute they'll be talking about one thing and before you know it, they'll be talking about something completely different. Conversations keep drifting around. There is no focus. People aren't tuned.

There is a way to tune our receivers to a wonderful station that has been playing since the beginning of time. This station actually makes creation. In the Bible there is a verse that says, In the beginning was the Word, and the Word was God, and the Word was with God, and everything that was made was made by the Word. Do you know that everything is vibrating? Everything is moving. You are made up of millions of teeny-weeny particles that are moving and dancing in lovely rhythms and harmonies. So is a chair, so is everything; the rugs, the walls, the ceiling, the air, anything you could name.

Scientists have blown up these little particles of matter bigger and bigger and bigger. They looked at the tiniest thing you could find, an atom, and they made it look huge. You know what? There was nothing there, nothing at all! The only thing they could find was something vibrating, something moving — a sound, a tone. This is just what the Bible said thousands of years ago, "In the beginning was the Word." It turns out that everything is a vibration. Everything is a sound. Everything is sound at different frequencies.

Let's make a deep note. If we could see this deep note, we could see that the waves are slow. Now let's make a higher note. If we could see the waves for this note we would see that they are faster, much faster. Now if we could see the waves for a chair, the atoms and molecules that make up the chair would be about twenty octaves above the range of our hearing. The chair is sounding a tone, but we can't hear it. The little atoms that make up everything are vibrating extraordinarily fast. Can you imagine a number with a one and fourteen zeros after it? It's a huge number. Every atom moves back and forth that many times each second.

And guess what else? The Earth itself is making a sound, but it's so deep we can't hear it. Scientists have noticed that every 53 minutes there is a teeny-weeny earthquake. The whole Earth is making a note! It's singing a song so deep that we don't notice it. If it stopped though, we'd probably notice it right away. The Sun vibrates too. All the planets vibrate. All the little atoms vibrate. It's all music. And we are a part of the music.

You are a note in a song and I am another note. If you strum a guitar, you play five or six notes all together and it sounds really good — a chord, right? Well, all of us here are a chord when we're vibrating right. In attunement we sound a beautiful chord. If the peoples of the world were all in attunement, they would be sounding music that we could actually hear. Some people actually do begin to hear the music that Life is playing throughout the universe. The stars, the planets, the galaxies are all vibrating to this song. This is the song of Life, the song of Creation. It is the Creative Word that was spoken in the beginning of time. It is still sounding. It is actually being spoken now. If we let ourselves come into attunement with that Creative Word, suddenly we are in harmony with all the people around us who are also tuned to that Creation station. And we don't have to try to make it happen. We let it happen.

The World is still being made.

Before the turn of this century, people who owned clock shops noticed something very curious. In those days you remember, most of the clocks had pendulums that swung back and forth. The people who repaired these clocks noticed that after a while all the pendulums would begin swinging back and forth together. Imagine working in a clock shop and one day noticing that all the pendulums were swinging together! They couldn't figure it out at first. So they experimented. They started up all the clocks at different times and sure enough, after a while all the pendulums would begin swinging together again.

Everything in nature wants to be in a state of harmony, in a state of swinging together with everything else. It happens for people when they let it happen. I'll bet that if we all forgot about it and just let our feet swing, soon they'd be swinging together. If we thought about it, we'd probably mess it up. But if we got to talking and didn't pay any attention to it, I'll bet that before we knew it, all our feet would be swinging together. Now what this means is really exciting.

When any one of us comes into harmony, it becomes easier for other people to come into harmony. In the clock shop they noticed that the more clocks there were with the pendulums swinging together, the harder it was to make one of them go different. It's like that with people. No, we're not all going to do the same thing. We're all different. We're all going to be doing something different. But it will be together, in harmony with what other people are doing — like different notes in a song.

The Creator is singing a song. It is love, but it is also vibration. Love turns into vibration when it comes in contact with truth. Truth is what matter is. When love and truth get together, we have the song of life. As people we are a part of that song. But behind the individuals that we are, we are also the one who is singing the song, a song that is bringing these forms into being. Fairly recently human beings decided to sing out of tune with the song of Creation that the whole rest of the universe is singing. This is why creation has stopped insofar as human beings are concerned. Creation has not been able to continue. What we see in the world today is not the end of the creative process that God started. This world is not a completed thing.

Chapter 3

DRESSED UP IN MATTER

Up until now God has made the universe from the out-side. The Creator sings and things happen. He sings a song about a tree and a tree grows — matter responds. But God does not have a spaceship, God does not have an exploratory vehicle, God does not have a body, or some-thing that He can get inside and still be completely awake. God wants to get dressed up in matter, to move around in matter, to begin to work with matter creating further forms from <u>inside</u>. He needs some instruments, some people who can hear His song and provide these waves of eternal life with something that can ride on their surface, reflect them and move with their energy. This will begin another level of creation, another kind of creation, a creation that will introduce things that are wonderfully beyond anything that we have ever imagined.

What is this like for the people who choose to work with God? It's like surfing. It's like riding wonderful waves that don't end at any shore. Waves that go on and on into eternity. We ride these waves on the surfboards of our bodies. We are not our emotions or our thoughts. We are more than that. We can stand on these things. We can stand on these vehicles and ride on these waves of energy, these beautiful currents of life that are moving out from that point where the universe began.

Many times people have an on-again-off-again experience. Have you ever noticed that some days you are in an easy flow? This is when you are balancing, riding on these surfboards that your body, mind, and heart could be compared to and having a wonderful time. But the next day you might be down in the dumps — you're crabbing or arguing with someone, having a bad time. You don't know how to stay on these surfboards yet. You haven't learned how to keep your balance.

Some of us have begun to ride these universal waves. We want to share with you what we have learned about keeping your balance. This is a most important thing to learn on this Earth. We want you to share this experience with us. That will make it even more fun and will make it easier for the people in our worlds to come into harmony with us.

The more people there are moving together in the current of Life, experiencing the joy of riding these eternal waves, the more fun it is for all of us. When there are enough of us doing this, something really magical is going to happen — more magical than I could even hint at. A transformation of the whole planet is going to take place.

Have you ever seen the moon reflected in a still lake? Isn't it beautiful? The reflection is sharp and clear. But if you throw a stone into that lake and make ripples, what do you see? You see a blur of light. You don't see the moon reflected very well at all. Well, that's what our world is like now. It's kind of like a blur. We know there is a light somewhere because there are signs that there is an awesome intelligence behind the scenes somewhere. But God's light looks blurry to human beings. It isn't being reflected clearly in their minds and hearts.

Attunement is a way of bringing people into a state where there is inner stillness and a clear reflection of God.

There are centers in the body where we sound a vibration that is in harmony with the deeper note that the Earth is sounding and the higher note that all the atoms are sounding. Attunement is exciting when you begin to experience it.

Remember the little creatures that live at the bottom of the ocean? Some of them went to the surface and learned to ride the great waves. Then they came down and tried to tell the others about this experience. There really isn't any way to explain attunement. Think of the times you had the most fun, the times when everything was flowing so well, maybe when you were ice skating, skiing or swimming, doing gymnastics, aerobics or sledding down a hill. Think of some of the best times you have ever had. Often they have to do with moving, with flowing with the forces of gravity, or with the music of a song. Think about those best times. These were times when you were in tune.

There is a way to have a good time always, not just on-and-off, on-and-off. When Jesus was on Earth He told us that we were to be the lights of the world. Each one is here to be a beacon, a beacon unto the world, not a strobe light that keeps going on and off. We are not here to flash on and off — some days on, having a good time, and other days off, not having a good time. We are here to be beacons, to be lights, to be shining stars. We are stars, you know. We really are stars. Stars express in different ways. In this age we have bodies to express through. Everyone of us can shine like the Sun. We can bring glorious light into this dark world. The world has been a miserable and sad place for many people. We can change that. There is nothing more exciting than learning about this process of attunement. We can have a good time all the time.

This is what Jesus tried to tell people. He said, "You can do it too. Don't just worship me — be like me. Be me.

Let the same spirit that I am move through you." And Jesus went around and did all kinds of miracles. He shared attunements with people in many different ways. One time He shared an attunement with a blind man and the man could see in an instant. People thought it was fantastic. They followed Him all over the place. They had never seen anybody who could make crippled people get up and walk or who could make blind people see. They followed Him around until finally Jesus said, "You know what? You can do all these things that I'm doing. You can do even greater things." The reason He said, "You can do even greater things" is because Jesus was all alone. He was like a single note sounding. He knew that if there were others who were vibrating with Him, if there were others who were making chords with Him, greater things could be done, much greater things, things that we can only begin to imagine.

We have a hint at what they might be when we look at the creation that has been possible in spite of people not helping. All the wonders you imagine are just a drop in a bucket compared to what will happen as people begin to come into attunement with God. It is already beginning to happen. We're seeing the beginnings of it. It might not be apparent to you children because you haven't had much experience in the old, decaying world that's falling apart. This is just as well. Hopefully you won't have to have much experience in that world.

Let's ride the current of these wondrous waves throughout each day wherever we go. As we let ourselves listen to them, they'll suggest to us what we might do with our time. This is the way God speaks to us. Soon we begin to see things we have never seen before.

RUACH

Hebrew for Spirit —

breath

wind

"waves of breath"

through God's breathing chaos becomes cosmos an orderly universe

Chapter 4

YOU ARE THE ONE THINGS COME TO

The reason the animals became wild is because people forgot that they would come all by themselves when they were supposed to. Before the Fall, the animals were different. There are even rumors that some of the animals could talk. People forgot that the animals would just come whenever they were needed. People began to chase after the animals and the animals became afraid of them. They didn't like to be chased. So the animals began running away.

The difference between the wild animals and the tame animals is whether or not they will come when you call them. If you begin to chase them, even your dog and cat won't come after a while. It's just like that with money, nice clothes, friends, toys, or any of the things that we want. If you chase them, if you try to get them, they don't come because you are not the real you then. Because the real you is not there. You are the one that things come to — that's who you really are. You are the one that things come to because you're the one who made the things. Things love to come to you. They love to be around you. They feel good just to be with you.

People often forget that money and all the nice things of this world are just like animals. When we chase them, they get scared. So how do we get these things we like? How do we get them to come to us? The secret is, we remember that they are like animals and we do the same that we would do with animals. We sit still, we don't chase after them, we are quiet, and we let them come. We remember that we're the one that made everything, then everything begins to come to us. It begins to come in the right way.

It helps to realize that all things have consciousness. They're smart. They think. They're like animals. They really are! People think that only animals and people can think. They think that grass is dumb. Most people would think that a piece of tin was worthless, but it's not, you know. If you really cared for it, if you took it home, treated it real nice and polished it up, you could look in it and see your face. You could hold it up and see the moon and stars at night. You could use it to reflect the Sun all over the walls and the ceiling. You could put it on a string and you could hang it around your neck. It could be something very special. Even an old scrap of tin has consciousness. There is nothing that doesn't. All things that people place value in have a certain kind of life that can be thought of in the same way we think of animals. Animals represent what we call the "subconscious" part of people.

When we talk together with our friends we use the conscious part of ourselves. But at night we go to bed and we have dreams. The dreams are often strange and mixed up. But it's still us, isn't it? We know it's us when we are having a dream, but it doesn't seem like us, does it? It seems bigger in a way, doesn't it? Have you ever had a dream that came true or that told you something that you found out later was right, that you didn't think you had any way of knowing?

When we're awake we think of ourselves as our mind or our body. But when we go to sleep we let go of all that; our consciousness expands out over our surroundings. We realize that everything we see is actually a part of ourselves. It's all inside of us.

Dreaming is a time when you get in touch with your larger self. Playing and drawing are other times when we let go of our identity, of who we think we are. There are other times too. While dreaming, our consciousness often drifts to touch the future. The close future isn't far away. It's not happening in another time. It's actually happening now. Everything that happens all really happens at the same time. It doesn't seem like it to us because we're inside of this, but everything that is happening all happens at the same time.

When we talk about the subconscious we are talking about a part of ourselves that most people don't have any idea is there; the dreaming part, our "dreamself." Little children tend to be more in touch with their dreamselves. As people get older, they forget about their dreamselves. They forget that there is that part of themselves. Then they get even bigger and then they start doing things to help them remember again.

There is a subconscious part of ourselves that knows everything without ever knowing why. When we connect up with that part of ourselves, then we are connected up with our whole subconscious. Do you know what our whole subconscious is? The whole world — and it's even more than that. But that is enough to keep us busy for now. Do you know what is in your subconscious? Everything—nice clothes, John Deere tractors, money, friends, trees, beautiful beds of flowers, ice cream and music. Everything is in your subconscious. It's all part of yourself and the things in it behave a lot like animals! When we connect up with that, and don't frighten the animals by chasing after them all the time, the ones that we are supposed to take care of come home to us.

There are certain things that need us. Even a John Deere tractor, for example, is smart. It's not a dumb

thing. It's like a sad little animal in a way, sad because it hasn't found the one that it needs to love it and take care of it. When you "let," when you just let everything be. When you don't try to go after things and you don't get all wrapped up in desires, so that you want this or that. "I've got to have this. I've got to have that. I'm going to try really hard so that I can get that." Whatever that thing is, when you just let it be, it may seem slow but very gradually when you stop chasing them, all the animals in the subconscious realm begin to peek out from behind the trees where they have been hiding.

They begin to look out from behind the bushes. The little squirrel says, "Psst! Psst!" to the tractor. "Look, they are not chasing things anymore. Peek out from behind that tree where you are hiding." And the John Deere tractor says, "I'm not hiding behind a tree, I'm hiding behind a barn." And the little squirrel says, "OK, peek out from behind the barn then. I think it is getting safer." And they look out, and all the other little animals begin to peek out too. The piano begins to peek out from behind the window in the piano store, or wherever it is hiding. All these things begin to peek out and they begin to watch you.

They are not going to come right away because as far as they're concerned, we've been acting crazy for a while. They are not quite sure that it's safe yet. So they're going to peek out. They're going to watch for a while. They're going to wait. Gradually they are going to slip up behind the next tree, a little bit closer and watch a bit more. But if we start wanting stuff really bad "Hey, gimme my book. Hey that's mine, that's mine, I want that" that scares them away. They go running right back to their hiding places again. Things don't come to us when we have that kind of attitude. Little children sometimes do that. That scares everything away. If we are quiet, those animals will peek out. They will begin to sense that it's safe. Little by little, they will come closer and closer and closer.

Did you know that everything in the world has been lost? It has been lost because we're the home and we've been lost! They don't know where we are. They don't know where to find us. People are supposed to provide a home for all the things in the world. But for the most part, people just act like smart animals; a bit smarter than some of the animals, but really not very smart at all. The animals don't see people calling them home, welcoming them. or taking care of them, so they feel lost and homesick. They're sad. We sometimes feel that sadness. It's the sadness of the whole world. The whole world is sad because it's homesick. It misses us. It misses you. When you're running around chasing after things it shows that you are lost.

Chasing things makes us part of the subconscious. We're not supposed to be part of the subconscious. We're supposed to be conscious. There's a big difference. The difference is between being awake and being asleep. People who are chasing things all the time are asleep, acting like lost and scared animals, running around in the dark. We have a chance to begin to understand this. We have a chance to begin to see that this whole world here is our subconscious. We are supposed to be the conscious part. There is a part of the world that is supposed to be subconscious. But people, human beings, are supposed to be the awake part. Through people the whole world can wake up. Now the whole world is sleeping. It's been sleeping for a long, long time. It wants to wake up. It's like somebody in a coma. It's more than a nap. There's something wrong. Sometimes people don't ever wake up from a coma, sometimes they just sleep and sleep until they die.

We need to wake up. And you know, each one of you can be just as important in waking up this world as anybody else. Each one of you is really important. Do you know how many people it would take to make this whole world wake up? One! Everybody thinks it would take everybody and people say, "Why should I bother?" But all by yourself you could do what is needed to wake this whole world. Anybody could.

Let's go back to the thought of sitting in the woods. We are all quiet. All the little animals are beginning to peek out from behind the bushes to see if it's safe. If we stay quiet they will come closer and closer and closer. But if we forget and get in some silly fight with somebody or some stupid argument, it will scare the animals right away again. We have to remember how important it is to be ourselves and to offer a loving welcome to all the things in the world, all the things that represent the subconscious part of ourselves.

We do this by taking care of the things that are closest to us. It's like magic in a way. We play our part toward making the world healthy by making sure that everything we do is right with everybody that we do it with, in every moment, no matter how little the thing. Everything is important. Every moment is important.

When we are still and quiet so that the things in the subconscious begin to peek out from behind the trees and bushes to see if it's safe, we begin to remember that it is safe too. And it feels so good! There's nothing on this Earth to scare us except our own reflection. Sometimes people start to be still. Then something begins to peek out from behind the trees and they look at it. They see the eyes glowing in the dark and they get scared, they think it's a monster. But what are they afraid of? They're afraid of their own dreams coming true! They have been so used to thinking about their dreams that they actually think they are happier in the dream. They are afraid to let go of their dreams so that the thing can really happen. When it begins to happen, it doesn't always look like it's beginning to happen.

Every time something happens to us that seems wrong, it is because our subconscious is trying to steer us in a different direction so that we can see something that we missed before. Every time it seems as though something bad is happening, it's only because we know something in our heart that we haven't quite been able to get through to our mind. Our heart is trying to say, "Hey, come on ahead, a little bit over this way, you'll see something. It'll change your whole life." There really isn't any such thing as something bad happening. It might seem bad but we need to remember that it's always a good thing if we have an easy attitude about it. We are happy that we know what we know.

Some people seem to have a lot of troubles. Other people hardly ever have troubles. Do you know what the difference is? It is the kind of thing we are talking about now — understanding. We are talking about understanding things that are very important, like the fact that nothing can ever really go wrong. Can you think of a time when something happened that seemed like it wasn't a good thing, but before it was over with you found out that because of that something wonderful happened. If the thing that seemed wrong hadn't happened, the wonderful thing would never have happened.

What if the training wheels got broken off your bike? It might seem bad, but because they were broken you would probably learn to ride your bike without them a lot sooner than if they were never broken. We all have training wheels on in different areas. Sometimes we get used to them and it isn't until we lose the training wheels that we find out that we can do without them. "Hey, I can do it! I can do it easy!'' Suddenly it is a whole lot better than when we had the training wheels on, though it seemed like a bad thing at first when the training wheels got broken. We can all do a lot more than we think we can do. In fact, we can all do anything we want. There is nothing that can stop us when we know who we are — the one things come to!

Chapter 5

THE WISHING TREE

There once was a boy who was taking a journey through the jungle. He had been traveling on foot for a long time and he was getting very tired. He saw a beautiful tree standing by the side of the road and he thought to himself, "This looks like a nice place to sit down and take a rest." So he sat down and leaned up against the tree to rest. "Boy, I sure am hungry," he thought. "I wish I had something to eat." The moment he thought of eating, instantly a big platter of delicious food appeared right in front of him. When he saw it he said to himself, "Hey, I'll bet this is the famous wishing tree! I must have sat down under the wishing tree!" After he ate the food, which was quite delicious, he sat back and thought, "I wish I had a bunch of toys to play with." Instantly there were toys all over the place. He thought that was really great! He had a tremendous time playing with all the toys. Then he thought, "Hey, I'm under the wishing tree. I can wish for anything I want." So next he wished for some ice cream and suddenly all the ice cream he could eat appeared before him. For the next little while he had the best time wishing for all the things he had ever wanted. But he had not been under the wishing tree very long before he thought, "Here I am all alone in the middle of the jungle. What if a tiger should come along and eat me?"

And it did.

The boy in this story couldn't be trusted with the wishing tree because he couldn't control his thoughts. As he thought about good things, the good things happened, but he didn't know how to keep himself from thinking about bad things. As soon as he thought about the first bad thing, it happened. The wishing tree was there to make his thoughts come true. Whatever his thoughts were, the wishing tree would make them come true. Would you like a wishing tree? Unless you know how to think only the right kind of thoughts, it would be just as well to not have a wishing tree. The good things you think come true, but the bad things you think come true also.

Having a body to drive around, having a mind like a fantastic radio that can generate and transmit thoughts, and having a heart to feel with, all this is quite new to you. It's not that often that you have a body and a mind and a heart. It's a new thing, having knees to look at, legs to walk around on. You are in a new land. There is a need to learn how to <u>be</u> in the right kind of way so that you don't continually make bad things happen to you. Whatever you put out comes back. It's very important to begin to see how true this really is.

For instance, the way to make sure your toys are safe is not by locking them up, but by behaving toward other people in such a way that what comes back to you will be the same thing that you put out. You can see this with your friends at school and with the people that you live with.

Sometimes it might seem as if you want to do certain things, but who you really are doesn't want to do those things at all. There's a part of yourself that gets ideas that you shouldn't listen to. Your real self always knows better. There is never a situation where you do something that is wrong, that you don't know that it is wrong in your heart.

Let you real self be the part that controls, the part that

decides. A child's mind is like a radio receiver. It picks up all kinds of thoughts, but you don't have to listen to all of them. They don't all reflect the real you. Many of them are not your thoughts at all. There are many ideas that come into your head that are not your ideas. You can always tell because there is something about them that just doesn't set right. If you begin to act on those ideas, you know that there's something wrong.

Until you remember who you are and why you came here and what you have to do, until you learn how to use your bodies, your minds, and your hearts in the way that you really want to use them, you need some training. You need some discipline, some rules. But the rules are really your own. They are rules that you made up a long time ago. You may not remember yet. They're here to keep you out of trouble until you remember.

Children love to learn. When it's something you are really interested in, you're eager to learn. When you stop to think about it, most of your time is spent learning. One of the most important things to learn is how to always have a good time. This involves a certain respect for other people.

In every moment you plant a seed of one kind or another. That seed is going to grow. If it is a seed of self-ishness, it is going to grow. If it is a seed of kindness, it is going to grow too. Which kind would you rather harvest in a few days?

You can't always see these seeds, but they are there growing all around you. You are in a jungle of things growing from seeds that you planted in the past. The plants that grow up in the jungle around you can be the kind of plants that have luscious fruit, the kind of plants that you can sit under and rest in their shade on a hot day, the kind of plants that can feed you, the kind of plants that you can climb, the kind of plants that you can

make things out of, the kind of plants that are friendly. Or they can be the kind of plants that trap you and have stickers and thorns and cause trouble. I'm talking about something that you can't see with your eyes, but it's very real. In fact, this invisible world that surrounds us is more real than the world we can see! The world that we see and touch needs to become as real as the invisible world that surrounds us. And this is what we are here on Earth to do.

You can't move through the world of doors and windows and houses and cars and schools and other people without also moving through an invisible world. You know that when you plant a seed in the garden, it grows. You know that if you leave your bicycle in the path you may trip over it coming back in the dark. Sometimes we leave things laying around in this invisible world. We leave things growing in this invisible realm that can either trip us up or help us. It is important to be aware of that.

The invisible world makes everything that we see in the real world the way that it is. The seeds that we plant in each moment grow first in this invisible magic world. And that is what sets up the pattern for the things in the world that we see and touch. So if you want things to be nice in the world that we see and touch and walk through, it is important that the things in this invisible world are right. We might not be able to see this invisible world, but our everyday experience can prove that it's there.

What messes up the invisible world more than anything else is wanting things. We might like to have all our good thoughts come true but we certainly wouldn't want all the bad things that pass through our minds to come true. But they do! We are under a wishing tree already. We really are. It's just that here in the world it takes a little longer, giving us more chances to learn what we

really want before it comes true. If we spend our time thinking right thoughts, right and enjoyable things will happen to us. If we spend our time thinking selfish thoughts, people will act selfishly toward us. If we are unkind, it will come right back to us. You reap what you sow. What you put out, you get back.

Did you ever get into the habit of always wanting something else? Always wanting something more? Children often get into that habit. And usually the more you get, the more you want. You can go on forever and ever and you'll never be happy because there's always more to get. Whether it's another bicycle or a couple of horses or whatever, people with that habit always want one more thing. Think about that for a while. As long as you want something you'll be unhappy.

You make a big hole in yourself when you want something. It's like a leak in the middle of your belly. All the happiness that should fill you up leaks out of that hole. As long as you want something, happiness runs out all over the ground. There is a wonderful life substance that keeps your heart beating and keeps you breathing. It fills you up in every moment. But when you want stuff, it leaks out. You are never satisfied when you are chasing after something. You're like a donkey with a carrot on a stick hanging in front of you. The donkey keeps walking trying to get the carrot, and the carrot keeps going farther and farther away because it's tied to a stick on the donkey's back. Every step the donkey takes, trying to get closer to the carrot, the carrot goes a step farther away. This is how the donkey's owner tricks him into following the carrot all over the place. But the donkey never catches up with the carrot because it's tied to his own back.

What we really want is to feel good. And the only way to feel good is to help other people feel good, knowing that as we plant good seeds, good seeds will come back to us. Then suddenly we're on a whole different kind of cycle. We seal that leak in ourselves. The happiness that flows into us in every moment has a chance to fill us up. We begin to feel right, we begin to feel comfortable, we begin to feel good.

People don't usually know what they really want. The boy or girl that can admit this, that can be honest about this and say, "You know, it's true, I don't always know what I really want," is a boy or a girl that can begin to appreciate the things we are talking about. If you can begin to see that what you think you want is only like scum on the surface of a pond, only the very top layer of what you really want, then what you really want can begin to come true. As what you really want comes true, a lot of the things that you thought you wanted come true too — in ways that you never imagined. But for this to happen, you have to stop wanting things and begin to be thankful for what you already have! It's amazing what you have right now if you stop to think about it. You have so much.

Let's be thankful for all that we have. Let's appreciate it. Then what really needs to happen can begin to happen. As we have a thankful attitude for what is already here, instantly new things begin to appear just like the animals peeking out from behind the trees when we are still. As long as we are wanting things we're stirring up scary things in the invisible world that chase all the things we want away. But as soon as we stop wanting things and give thanks, then we're like a little child in the middle of the forest who sits still long enough for the animals to begin to peek out from behind the trees. They begin to creep up very slowly, very softly. They want to be your friend, but they are afraid to be friends with somebody who wants. They know that somebody who wants will always be wanting something more and will soon forget about them.

You have to be pretty mixed up to think that you're going to get what you want by breaking the rules. They are your own rules, there to remind you how to get what you really want. More than anything else, don't you want to feel good? Do you feel good when you do things that you know aren't right? You feel pretty bad, don't you? When you don't have your own approval it's impossible to feel good. That's a big word — approval. Do you know what it means? It means "being friends." Now there's something much bigger than any one of us that we need to be friends with. We've called that God. When we are friends with God, we feel good and life is good to us. Life supports us, life helps us, life fills our every need.

We are all under a wishing tree. Think about that. In the Bible, we're told that this can either be the exciting, wonderful, adventurous Tree of Life or it can be the Tree of the Knowledge of Good and Evil — the Tree that leads to misery and troubles and sorrows. It all depends on how you use it.

Whenever thoughts come into your head, just think, what if they came true instantly? There is some protection around the traps that are in this Earth where you've landed. You have a little time (childhood is what it's called) to learn to use your body, your mind, and your heart as the Tree of Life. Someday you won't have the protection that you have now. Everything that you think will come true. I know that you are all able to think wonderful thoughts. I know that you can create tremendous things. I'd like to see you do it!

Chapter 6

SOME OF US MAY REMEMBER . . .

In the beginning there was a bright, bright light and that light was God. One day that light decided that it would be fun to have other lights to play with. So that light, because it was God and could do anything, became several lights. Each one of those lights was a spirit. We know that we are spirits. Do you know what God is? God is one single being who chooses to become as many beings, while still remaining one at the source, like a tree. A tree has many leaves but they are all part of one tree. When Jesus was on Earth He said, "I am the vine and you are the branches." God is an organization of God beings. We are some of those beings that are God.

In the beginning we were with God and we created the universe, all the stars in the sky, all the planets, the moon and the Sun. We wanted there to be some people who were made out of the same kind of substance that the planets, the moons and the stars were made out of — people who could reflect us in the universe and on the Earth that God had made. So we made the first man, Adam, and the first woman, Eve, in our image and likeness. We made the first people to look like us — designed them so that they could reflect us. They were special kinds of mirrors that could reflect the light that we were, that could think our thoughts on the Earth that we had made, and that could love the animals, the trees and the little creatures that were on this world.

It is kind of like a costume party. Because we were light, we didn't have any clothes to wear. We were eternal spirit. We had made a universe to clothe a certain part of ourselves, but not the real playful part of ourselves, not the part of ourselves that we really enjoyed being the most. To put clothes on the part of ourselves that we really liked the most needed something very special. The stars, the suns, the planets and the moons, could all be nice clothes for certain parts of ourselves. But the conscious part of ourselves (the part that sings and dreams, creates and designs, plays and plans) needed something more than just a moon or a planet or a star spinning around in space to clothe it. So we created people. We created human beings. Some of us may remember that. Certain people remember it easier than others sometimes. But when that happened, we were like a tree at the trunk that hadn't branched out yet, we hadn't branched out yet into branches, leaves and buds.

So we made these people. We came down out of heaven, out of the higher vibrational channels. Do you know that we live on channels like the channels on a television set? On a television set you can tune to one channel or another channel, but all the channels are in the same place. Which one you pick up depends on how you have the set tuned. It's the same way with Heaven and Earth. Right now there are many different channels, many different vibrational levels. We're tuned into one channel right now. But there are other channels. We need to learn how to turn the dial. The dial on our human set has been stuck for twenty thousand years on this one channel because something happened to people and the channel changed and got stuck that way. Most people don't realize this. They think that this is the only way it can be. But it isn't. It's just one of many ways, and it's not necessarily the best way.

In the beginning we created the human creatures so that we could have exploratory ships to explore the surface of planet Earth, so that we could have instruments to ride around in, and do things, build things and make things. As we began to move from the trunk of this Tree of Life, we began to branch out into different aspects of one self, and we began to start having friends. It was really fun to see different parts of ourselves dressed up in different ways, to see our friends dressed up in different shapes, different bodies, and different minds.

But then something went wrong. You've probably heard of the Fall. In the Bible it tells of Adam and Eve eating the fruit of a tree that they weren't supposed to eat fruit from. Have you ever seen a chart that shows the human nervous system? It touches every cell in your body and looks very much like a tree. At the top of that tree is your brain which is part of the nervous system. It is like the uppermost part of a tree branching out with the roots running down throughout the rest of the body. That tree in us is supposed to be our instrument — something that we use to bring life into the Earth. That is why it is called the Tree of Life. But when the serpent (or the identity that lived in that tree) started doing its own thing, started deciding what was good and what was evil, then the human creatures began eating the fruit of that tree. They started having ideas of their own. The part of ourself that was in them became lost in their dream. This wrong channel got clicked on and has been stuck on ever since. Things got worse and worse and worse. From a beautiful garden, the world degenerated into a dangerous and scary place.

About 2,000 years ago we managed to get a message through to these lost creatures who had forgotten all about us. A person whom we call Lord of Lords and King of Kings, the One who started everything, the One at the very middle of the trunk of the Tree of Life, was able to change the channels on the body of a man named Jesus. He was able to get the body, the mind and the heart of this man named Jesus to do what he wanted him to do. This was the first time in thousands of years that anyone of us God beings was able to get a human creature to respond to our light. We hoped that Jesus would explain what was going on to the people who were on Earth so that they would stop paying attention to all the things that were going on in their bad dreams, and remember us — the light of God that was inside them!

Jesus explained to people what had happened and what they needed to do to let it all be right again, so that all the killing, hunger, sorrow and disease, could be ended and people could begin to have a good time again. But the people didn't understand what Jesus came to say. They crucified Him and put Him in a tomb under the ground with a big stone at the mouth of it. They dressed Him in the grave clothes in which they dressed dead people. Jesus was in the tomb like people in the world are in a tomb right now, dead to the conscious part of themselves — asleep.

The story of Jesus is important because it is the story of the whole human race. The story of Jesus is the story of us all. After He was in the tomb for three days, Jesus woke up. An angel of the Lord rolled the stone away from the mouth of the tomb. Jesus took off the grave clothes and walked out of the tomb into the garden. There was a lady in the garden named Mary who was sad because she thought that Jesus was dead. On Easter Sunday morning she came to the garden, to the tomb where his body lay, to cry and to think about Him. As she was walking through the garden she saw a man standing there. She had tears in her eyes. She didn't recognize who it was.

She thought the person was a gardener. But you know who the person really was? It was Jesus — all shining and full of light. So Mary asked Him, "What have they done with my Lord?" because she wanted to know where Jesus was. And Jesus just said, "Mary." She could hardly believe it was Jesus, but it was.

We are at this point right now in human history. The human race has been in the tomb for three days. For the last little while, about 2,000 years, the human race has been waking up subconsciously. You know how before you actually wake up, you begin to wake up way down deep? You wake up little by little, closer and closer to the surface, so that by the time you really wake up and open your eyes, you've already done a lot of waking up down in your heart. So for 2,000 years now, which isn't really that long compared to the 20,000 years that the human race has been in the tomb, we've been waking up inside and we're in the last few minutes now. We're beginning to wake up consciously. We're beginning to remember things that people have not remembered since the beginning.

We're beginning to remember things that have been forgotten since the fathers fell asleep, since Adam and Eve ate the fruit of the Tree of the Knowledge of Good and Evil And because we're beginning to remember these thing ᵢ, the angels that we really are, are able to blend with these sleep-walking forms, these human creatures that have been staggering around in the darkness for so long. Something is happening now, something as wonderful as when Mary came into the garden to see what she thought was going to be the dead body of Jesus and instead found a shining radiant being of light — almost too bright to look upon. Remember in the story when she started to hug Jesus, Jesus said, "Don't touch me."? If Mary had touched Him at that point it would have been like touching an electric fence because Jesus had taken off the grave clothes.

The grave clothes are the thoughts and the ideas that people have that are so grave and so serious and so heavy. People think heavy thoughts, serious thoughts. But we need to take them off. When we do we become lighter. The word "grave" means the tomb — death — right? The word "grave" also means serious, doesn't it? The word "gravity" means something that pulls us down to the Earth and sticks us to the ground. When we begin to take our thoughts lightly, when we begin to take everything lightly, when we begin to take off the grave clothes, then we become lights and we become light. It would be nice to fly, wouldn't it? Gravity is a useful thing, but we were never meant to be bound by it. We were meant to have dominion over the Earth. Think about that, dominion over the Earth. This has something to do with sailing in the air of spirit. Air is the symbol of spirit. Spirit is what we are. Spirit is what God is. Spirit is what blows through all these forms. If we could see spirit, we could see spirit blowing through the trees, blowing through the grasses, blowing through each one of us. Spirit is what we are. And spirit knows. Spirit knows everything.

Spirit knows how beautiful this world can be. Spirit knows how light these forms could be if the owners of the vehicles would take them lightly. As long as we take ourselves so seriously and our problems and wants so seriously, we are heavy. The reason the angels can fly is because the angels take themselves lightly.

Chapter 7

A WAVE OF AWAKENING

If you were an unlit light bulb and all your friends were unlit light bulbs, and you went through your whole life being with other light bulbs that weren't lit, you might never know that there was such a thing as a lit light bulb. It would be fun to do a puppet show with a bunch of light bulbs. They could have different names and we could put faces and hats on them. We could pretend that they were friends and have them talking to each other. But what a difference when one of those light bulbs gets connected up to its source. What a difference when one of those light bulbs allows the current to flow through it. It's a whole different thing, isn't it? You know what? I'm going to tell you something really funny, it's funny but it's sad. You know why the light bulbs in this story won't let themselves be lit? Because they are afraid of the dark! They are so afraid of the dark that they don't trust the electricity that would light them up. Yet darkness is all they have ever known.

Now this is just a story of course, a parable, but it's the same with people. People are like light bulbs that have never been lit up. There is something that we can connect with that will light us up. It's hard to imagine, isn't it? Our spirits are already lit up. But these bodies and these minds, these things that think up here on our shoulders have got some bad habits — old habits that go back a long way and keep us from letting the current flow. We know that a light bulb has to be screwed into a socket to make it light up, but people are already screwed into the sockets. All we have to do is let the juice begin to flow through us. We have been resisting. We've been pushing life out. When life really begins to flow through us, it's kind of like surfing — suddenly woosh! We're riding away on something tremendous. The body and the mind have been a little scared of that. "What do you mean woosh? I don't know if I want to go woosh!" But it's here now — a tremendous wave moving through the Earth. Do you know what that wave is? It's a wave of awakening. It has been on its way for 2,000 years.

When there is a tidal wave out in the ocean, the scientists will calculate how fast it's coming and they'll tell the people, "There is a tidal wave coming. It's going to reach your shores in 2 days." And most of the people get ready, but some of the people don't believe the scientists. "Ah, scientists don't know what they're talking about. It's a sunny day, it's peaceful, the ocean is calm. There's not going to be any tidal wave." But the smart people prepare for the coming of the tidal wave. Do you know what a tidal wave is? It's a huge wave as high as a mountain. It comes roaring in from the sea because of a great storm. It knocks over buildings and washes away cars. It has a tremendous power.

Well, this wave of awakening that is sweeping through the collective consciousness of human beings started when Jesus Christ burst through the tomb, rolled the stone aside, took off the grave clothes, and began to shine. That was what started the tidal wave. A man who was very close to Jesus, named John, warned the people, "There's something coming and you had better prepare." And it's true. A collective awakening is going to occur when suddenly what happened in Jesus (the light bulb lighting up) would start happening — pop . . . pop . . . pop . . . all over the place. All of a sudden, in one generation from the time it began happening, it would sweep the whole human species.

Well it's happening. It's happening right now. You are seeing people beginning to glow — probably just a slight glow — but you're beginning to see people glow. You'll see them get brighter and brighter and you'll see more and more people begin to glow. Something wonderful is happening. Fortunately the lights don't just pop on. People have lived in the dark for so long that if the lights just popped on all at once it would be too much for people to handle. So, thanks to God, the light goes on bit by bit, like one of those lights with a knob that you turn up very slowly.

The light is on in our world today — no matter how bad things may seem — and the knob is being turned up slowly. There is nothing that is going to stop it. It is going to be turned up more and more. The lights are going to get brighter and brighter until all darkness is filled with light. The dark days of all those little light bulbs will soon be ended. Light bulbs either have to light up or disappear. People have to light up or die. There's no middle ground. There's no sitting on a fence, no half in and half out.

This process has been called the Second Coming of Christ, it has been called the Last Judgment, and it has been called other things as well by other cultures. It has been well-known that a time would come when this would begin to happen. And I really want you young people to know that it is happening now. And there is no turning back. We've got no choice as a species but to wake up. And it's about time! There are four and one-half billion people in the Earth right now, four and one-half billion people and they are all like unlit light bulbs. The ones that are beginning to light up are trying to tell the other ones how easy it is to simply let themselves be lit.

Shadrach, Meshach and Abednego lived a long time ago. They believed in God and trusted Him. This made the king of the land in which they lived angry. One day he said, "Shadrach, Meshach and Abednego, I want you to bow down and worship this pretend god that I made." Shadrach, Meshach and Abednego said, "No way. We know God and we will only worship the one God." (Worship means listen to, pay attention to, be one with). "We're going to be one with the only God," they said. "The heck with your pretend God." And the king said "All right, if you don't worship this false God, I'm going to put you in a hot furnace." Shadrach, Meshach and Abednego said. "Well, do whatever you think you have to do, but we're sure not going to worship your pretend god."

So the king had the guards throw as much wood as they could into this furnace. He had the fire heated seven times hotter than it had ever been heated before. The king tied them up and ordered the guards to throw them into this fiery furnace. When the guards carried them to this furnace, it was so hot that the guards had no sooner thrown Shadrach, Meshach and Abednego in when they were burned up themselves because the fire was so hot. Shadrach, Meshach and Abednego landed in the middle of this roaring fire. From a good ways off the king looked in the furnace to see what was going on, and he couldn't believe his eyes. He saw Shadrach, Meshach and Abednego walking around in the furnace singing a little song. The ropes that the king had tied them with had burned right up. They were free. Then the king was even more astonished to see a fourth person in the fire. He had only thrown three in. But there was another person in there. The fourth person was like unto the Son of God.

This is what happens when the light bulbs light up. Shadrach, Meshach and Abednego represent your body, your mind, and your heart. They have to enter the fire. They have to let themselves be lit up seven times hotter than they have ever been heated before. I'm sure that a 100 watt bulb, if it's screwed in, is at least seven times hotter than it was when it was sitting in the drawer. Your body, you mind, and your heart have to be heated through the fire of God's love seven times hotter than they have ever been heated before. Then the bonds that hold you will be burned away.

When those three parts of yourself are changed in the fire, then the fourth, like unto the Son of God, the angel that you really are, will be able to enter your facilities wholly and completely, and will be able to use your body, mind, and heart as they were designed to be used. Once again, you, as you really are, will have full control of your facilities. Like a shining light, with a body of light, you will have dominion over the Earth. You and your friends will be dressed in costumes much more delightful than these coarse crude costumes that we are dressed up in today.

This is the story of Easter. Do you know what the fire represents? It represents love. Love is the most exciting thing there is. You can feel love for one very special person. You can feel love for many special people. Or you can feel love for all people, for every rock and every stone and every blade of grass, every tree and every pebble and every cloud. Turning on the love is how we turn on the current that lights us up. Sometimes in the beginning it takes one very special person to show us that we have the power to turn that switch on. And that's all right. But once we learn that the switch is there, we learn that we can turn it on any time at all! And as we turn on the current, we begin to glow. The fire within burns brighter.

And the bonds that hold us, the grave thoughts, are all burned away. We're free to be who we are, to do what we came here to do, to watch all our dreams come true.

We've had wonderful dreams. If we told them to our special friend, our special friend might say, "Impossible!" But we know in our hearts that our dreams can come true. They come true when we turn on the current of love and begin to love everything as much as we can. That's what it's all about. It is very simple really. Most people have forgotten where the knob is that changes the channels. Turning on the love increases our vibrational frequency. In the Bible the Creator speaks of "quickening life." "I will quicken your spirit."

Long ago, children, you and I quickened the first life on this planet. But then something happened. Human beings forgot about us and started doing their own thing. Now we have come back to re-establish dominion. We're here to return the Earth to the Lord.

Chapter 8

CHRISTMAS MORNING
FOR THE FAMILY OF MAN

The reason God gave the Ten Commandments to Moses was because people had forgotten to be what they were created to be. If people remembered who they were, they wouldn't need commandments. To be in agreement with God is an easy and natural condition. When people forgot, everything got complicated. So God gave the children of Israel Ten Commandments. Commandment means rule — ten rules. These were to help the people remember what they should have always known. They were to help the people behave in such a way that they would once again remember what they had forgotten.

One of the rules was given to young people. It goes like this: "Honor your father and your mother that your days may be long in the land which the Lord God has given you." The land that the Lord God has given you is your own body. Have you ever thought about that? You own land. Each one of you has a piece of the rock! Each one of you is the king or the queen of a wonderful country — your body. Because of your body, you have this magical realm called your mind in which wonderful stories and adventures can take place. And you have this exciting realm called your heart which can also share in these stories and adventures. So each of you is the king or the queen of a magical country. Wouldn't you like your days to be long in this land that God has given you? The way your days get to be long in the land that God has given you is by honoring your father and your mother.

Your father and your mother are the two parts of the River of Life. Your father is Love, symbolized by the Sun. Love is the current, the energy that pushes the water down the river. Your mother is the Truth, the water that flows into the sea of eternal being. Do you see the difference? If you just had water sitting still in a pond you wouldn't have a river.

Life is a flowing river. The water is your mother, the Earth. The current of the father, the Sun, is moving through it, washing over it always loving it, moving it along. In a time-lapse movie of a flower growing, you can see the flower growing very quickly. Soon it blossoms, turns brown and withers back into the dirt. If you had enough film, you could take a time-lapse movie of a tree. You could show a tree sprouting up from a little acorn. You could show it growing bigger and bigger. You could show woodpeckers pecking holes in it. You could show the owls coming and living in it. You could show it getting older and older and the branches starting to fall off and lightning striking it. You could show it dying and the branches falling off, and it all turning back into sawdust. You could show all that in 10 seconds. It might begin to remind you of waves, of a river, of something flowing.

If we had enough film and enough time, we could take time-lapse movies of the Himalayan Mountains which weren't even there forty or fifty thousand years ago. We could show them growing and then falling away again. We could take movies of everything on Earth, trees, forests, grasses, flowers, oceans, mountains and rivers. We would see that this whole Earth is flowing and moving and bubbling, a planet slowly boiling in the rays of the Sun. The Earth is alive and changing. Our Father is the energy that moves through the Earth. The Earth is the Mother representing the truth of the universe. Before the Father came to the Earth there weren't any trees or grasses. But as the fire of the Sun washed over the Earth, Sun and Earth became one, and began expressing what we call Life — this bubbling river of Life.

If we want our days to be long in this magical land the Lord God has given us, if we want to know how to use the wonderful country of our minds in the way that Life intended, we need to begin honoring and respecting the Earth and the Sun, and the love and truth which they represent. Our earthly father and our earthly mother also represent love and truth. We need to cooperate with them too and work with them. They are here to help us learn how to drive these wonderful exploratory ships that we live in while we are on Earth. Unless we honor our father and our mother, we will never learn how to control our capacities and they will never be able to reflect us here in form.

It is important to listen when you're told to do a chore or a certain task. Pay attention, listen and try to understand. Your earthly parents are your friends. They are here to help you learn how to enjoy this magic country that you live in. You probably don't remember, but you picked them yourself.

Right now you are choosing everything that happens to you. There is nothing that happens to you that you didn't decide to make happen. If you get sick, you made it happen. If you get a wonderful present on your birthday, you made it happen. If you get a nosebleed, you made it happen. Everything that happens to you, you make happen.

Most people and most children make things happen subconsciously. They are not in control. It is just kind of happening as a dream. If we put gas in a car, started it up, put a brick on the gas pedal and gave it a push in the pasture, it would probably run around for a while. Suppose you were sitting in the back seat looking out the rear window! The car would be running around all over the place. Well, there's energy there — the power of the subconscious. The power of the emotional creative realm is there, but it's choosing its experience randomly. Nobody's steering. Do you think your days in the back seat of the uncontrolled car are going to be long? More than likely, it's going to crash into a tree pretty quick. There will be nothing for you to do but crawl out and go looking for another car. That one will be worthless!

It is the same with these bodies, minds and hearts that we live in. We need to learn how to drive them. We need to learn how to be the ones that are in control of them, so that they're not just running us all over the place every time they want a candy bar or a new train set. So many people get run all over the place because of their likes and dislikes. Somebody says something to them and they feel horrible. Somebody else says something to them and they feel good. Are we being run all over the place by things that are happening outside in the world around us? Are we thinking that we're something separate from the river, and not seeing that we really are in control?

Trying to make everything good happen can still be part of thinking that you are the ripple instead of the river. When we realize that we are the river and not the ripple in the river, then we don't have to make anything happen because we already ARE at a point of oneness with the river. Before we can decide to make certain things happen, we go through a learning process where we begin to let things happen. You see, we've been out of touch. We have been thinking that we were our bodies. We've been out of touch with this current that is moving through everything. To get back in touch with that again, we have to let go of all the things that make us think we are separate from the river. We have to let things happen for a while. When we let things happen for a while, we gradually find that our identity becomes one with all of life. Then when we know who we are, when the angel that we are is fully able to live in this land, then we can choose what we're going to let happen. But first we have to make sure the usurper is no longer in control.

There has been a pretend person in your own body and mind, trying to run things, a person who isn't real, a person who believes lies, who thinks he is separate from life, who thinks that he can be made happy in a selfish kind of way, that doesn't take into account the whole. Fortunately, the good king can come back and the land can become happy again. The pretend king needs to be sent away. He has a place, but it isn't in charge of the kingdom, that's for sure!

If the people in this land are to be happy, if our bodies are to be healthy, we have to say "No" to the pretend person that says, "I want this, I want that!" We have to say, "No way!" This mind and this body are here to be used by me, by the truth of my spirit, by the reality of what I AM. This is the only way we can begin to experience the adventures that are here for awakened children of God. We have been asleep while the false king ran the show. But we're beginning to wake up now. The angel is entering these forms much more fully. As we wake up, we're beginning to notice something mighty interesting, mighty exciting. All of a sudden something inside of us remembers, "Hey! It's Christmas morning!" Our eyes pop wide open! There's no way we are going back to sleep again!

This is Christmas morning for the family of man. This is the first Collective Christmas. Christ has been waiting to incarnate on Earth for a long time.

Do you know what incarnate means? It means to get dressed up in matter. We've been dressed up in bodies of light many times before, but we thought it would be fun for a change to get dressed up in matter, in these dense physical bodies so that we can raise them up into the light so that each and every cell of these bodies can share our eternal life. We live forever. We always were and we always will be. You have always existed and always will. The river lives forever! The little whirlpools come and go. They fade in and they fade out depending on the amount of rain. This Christ-awakening is something we've been looking forward to for a long time.

What a sense of appreciation we have for these bodies, minds and hearts that enable us to broadcast on this level, sending out signals that will wake up all the other children in this sleeping realm. We're waking up and we're remembering. We made these plans together long ago, you and I. We are eternal partners in this dance. We decided we were going to do this. We knew that when we dove into this material plane there might be a tendency to forget some things. So we made a pact, a secret deal with each other that when we got here we'd help wake each other up again. That's why we are sharing these words today, so that we can all wake up and go out and wake up the rest of our friends. We've got a lot of friends here. Most of them are sleeping. Let's wake up ourselves and then let's wake up the rest of our friends and tell them the glorious news, that it is Christmas morning, that is is the beginning of a new age, a new cycle of adventure and creation when wonderful and magnificent things are going to happen. No adventure story that you could ever imagine would even be a hint of what we are going to experience in this eternal life together.

Chapter 9

I AM THE RIVER

Let's be quiet for a moment and think about where we come from. We have an earthly parent and we have a heavenly parent. These bodies that we live in are a sort of shadow of what we are — a shadow cast in the Earth. Remember the one light that became many lights? The part of the light that each one of us is, is what we call the angel. The angel is like an airplane flying over the ground on a sunny day. It makes a shadow on the Earth. The angel causes all of the substance of the Earth (the mud, the rocks, the clay, the stones, the gravel) to rise up, like a magnet might lift a pile of iron filings. The angel that we are comes down to the Earth and stuff from the Earth starts to come up. If you hold a magnet under a piece of paper, scatter some iron filings on the paper and shake them around, the filings will arrange themselves in a pattern. This pattern will show you the magnetic field around the magnet. The angel that we are has a field around it too. As it comes close to the Earth, particles are lifted up from the Earth just like a magnet would lift up iron filings. Our bodies are formed to clothe that angelic field. But we are the field. We are the light. We are the part of God that moves into the Earth and dresses itself in these forms.

If you ever watch a river flowing, especially after a flood when the water is high, you'll notice many little ripples and whirlpools. In some places, maybe where a rock is buried beneath the surface of the river, the water will make very interesting patterns. You can watch these patterns. Sometimes the patterns will look like little horses' heads. Other times they will look like bumps. They will take all kinds of strange shapes.

When water moves rapidly over something it makes strange patterns in the water. When you look at these patterns they look like things, but what are they? What are they really? They're made out of the water. But what is the water doing? Flowing. Every second these shapes are made out of completely different drops of water. So even though there is a shape there, what is it really? It can't be the water. The water keeps moving on. It isn't rock, though the rock under the surface may be causing it. It is something else. There is a pattern there of some kind. Now in a way, people are like ripples and whirlpools in the flowing current of Life. In the beginning was a creative act. Something began to flow like a river. As this river flows here and there, it makes these interesting patterns.

It seems that people are detached from the Earth. We don't have roots like a tree. We can actually walk around. It seems that we aren't connected to other people. After all, we can't see anything connecting us. We can jump. We can run. But even though it may appear that we aren't connected to the Earth or to each other, our roots are as deep and as necessary as a tree's. We couldn't live very long in these bodies if we got very far away from the Earth.

Now what happens is that people begin to think that they are their bodies. And this is a lie. It's something that is not true. It is something that we need to understand because as long as we think that we are our bodies we'll never know who we really are. It would be like that little whirlpool in the stream thinking that it was something all of itself. Suppose that little whirlpool thought it was a person. Well, the water keeps flowing through it. In one minute it is made up of certain drops of water. In the next minute it is made up of completely different drops of water.

You can see the mistake that the whirlpool in the river would make if it thought of itself as something apart from the river. It's not anything apart from the river. It's an expression of the whole river, a part of the river. In fact it is the river. A lot of water flows through that ripple. If you collected all the water that flows through that ripple, you'd find that you could probably fill up a whole pond very quickly. The whirlpool is really a projection of the whole river. If it thought of itself as just a pattern in the river, it would limit itself to a very short, tough life. It's the same with people. When people think that they are just their bodies, they're making a big mistake. They are much more. It is the pattern of the angel that causes the Earth flowing through to form into these shapes. We are more than the shapes. To begin with, we have something called a mind and a heart. The mind is the part with which we think, the part with which we tell stories, and the part with which we listen to stories. The heart is something that we feel with, that we love with, that we express emotions through. The mind and heart are connected closely with the body. If it wasn't for the body, there wouldn't be any mind or any heart in the way that there is. So we're not our minds either. We are not what we think. We are not the thoughts that we think or the ideas that we have. We have a name for ourselves but we're not that either, not that at all. Those are just the words that we pin (like we might pin a tail on the donkey) on this ripple, this pattern that the angel makes when the angel flies through the Earth.

The cells in your body don't live forever. Every so often they are completely replaced. In fact, every seven years you have a whole new body. The body you are now in is not the same body with which you started. By the time people are 14 years old, they're on their third completely different body. This is like the water flowing through the ripple in the river.

Did you know that we are actually flying? We are moving beings! We are part of this enormous flow, yet we are the whole thing as well. We express as different kinds of ripples in different people. But we really are the whole thing. I once saw a joke where there was this little fish swimming around and there was this other fish that was supposed to be his teacher. The little fish swam up to this teacher fish and he said, "Where is this ocean that you keep talking about? I don't think there really is any ocean!" Of course both the fish were in the ocean, but because it was everywhere the fish that was learning didn't think that there was any such thing. All he was looking at was the other fish and the bottom of the sea and the shells and the sand. He was so focused on all those things that he never even knew that there was an ocean that he was in.

Have you ever heard the expression, "You can't see the forest for the trees?" Do you know what that means? Say you are standing at the edge of a wood and you are looking at individual trees. You are looking at the trees so hard you don't see the forest. It's kind of like that with people on Earth today. They are looking at so many specific things; they are looking at so much detail they don't even notice this tremendous river of life that is washing over the Earth changing everything in its path.

The angel that each one of us is, comes into this Earth to be reflected in these bodies, minds, and hearts. This angel is an aspect of the whole current, part of the whole flow. It takes the whole river to make each little ripple. You might say, "Well, the river is pretty wide and that one little ripple just takes up just a few feet right over here." But if you took away any of the water in the river, it would change the pattern of the whole river and that ripple would be completely changed. There is no way that you could change anything in the river without changing everything in the river. There is no way you could lift out one of those little ripples somehow and hold it off to the side while the rest of the river flowed by. Yet that's what people try to do with their lives. They try to lift themselves out of the flow. They try to separate themselves. They think that, "I am just this body, just this mind, just this heart. I am going to be selfish and I am going to get the things that I want. I'm going to ignore everybody else." It just doesn't work that way. It can't work that way. When people try to do that, the law comes into effect.

The law is this: you reap what you sow. When you act selfishly, you become subject to other people's selfishness. This is what everybody on Earth has been doing since the beginning of time. The pattern needs to be broken. Thinking they were their bodies, minds and hearts, people imagined that they could do whatever they wanted. People have thought that they could be selfish and get away with it. But they can't. Since Adam and Eve ate the fruit of the Tree of Knowledge of Good and Evil, people have been doing this and people have been dying. The shadows of the angels — the bodies, minds and hearts — have been getting ideas of their own. The shadows have been saying, "I don't want to reflect the angel. I would rather reflect the dirt and the mud, the rocks, the earth and clay from which I was made." So the shadows quickly fade after a few decades and fall back into the Earth as the angel moves on and tries to find a shadow somewhere who wants to be friends.

It is important that we, as angels, teach these bodies, minds and hearts how to reflect what we are. We have to learn how to drive these bodies. We have to learn how to operate them. If we don't, we're as dangerous as a person driving a car who doesn't know how to steer.

Do you think it would be fun to drive a backhoe? What if you climbed on one right now and started it up? You'd have a heck of a time trying to run the thing without knowing how. You'd probably pick up the bucket on the front end and accidently knock over the house. Maybe you'd pick yourself out of the seat with the claws and drop yourself onto the compost pile. It could really be a mess if you didn't know how the controls worked. Well, that's kind of the way it is with these bodies, minds and hearts. The angel needs to learn how to control them. The angel needs to be the one who is in charge.

Each angel, each God being, is a fragment or an aspect of the one light. Each one of us is a tiny golden flickering. Have you ever seen a big bonfire outside at night? You notice how certain flames detach themselves? You might see a piece of a flame all by itself. If we took a slow motion movie of the bonfire, we would see pieces of flames unconnected. They would look like they were unconnected but they'd still be part of the one fire. It's kind of like that with the angels that we are. There is one God who always lives at the heart of the fire. That is our essential being behind all being. In this time we are interested in representing different parts of that one central being. The little flames that we are, are connected to that being and in agreement with it. Each angel is in agreement with the central God being and in agreement with every other angel.

When the body, with its mind and heart, allows itself to be controlled by its angel, then it is in a state of cooperation and harmony with every other person who is also letting his or her body be controlled by the angel that he or she is. How do you get the body to do what the angel wants it to do? It requires discipline in the beginning. It requires education and training. Powerful bad habits have been established in collective human consciousness. Children are often prone to these bad habits and their parents are here to help them learn how to run the bodies that they've got. Most children don't know how to drive themselves. They really haven't learned how their equipment works. So they run all over the place and they listen to every little thing that the body wants, every little thing that the mind wants. They get upset and they experience emotions that are uncomfortable. Their parents represent the Sun, the Earth, the Love and the Truth that made all this. Parents represent God. Parents can help teach their children how to drive their bodies and how to be in control of their minds and hearts. Then when the children grow up and leave their parents, they know how to operate their equipment and they can do whatever they want to do in life.

It is foolish for the whirlpool in the river to imagine that it is something separate from the river. And it's just as foolish for people to imagine that they can somehow go their selfish way while ignoring everybody else. You are everything that you see! Did you know that? Everything that you touch, everything that you feel, everything that you hear is all a part of you. The chairs in your room, the people, the rocks, the grasses, the trees, the clouds in the sky, the backhoe, the tractor, the cars, the food you eat, is all YOU. It's all part of this river that you are.

God has a wonderful surprise for anyone who will stop thinking of themselves as just their own little part of things and begin thinking of themselves as this whole field of movement, this whole river. The surprise is that you can then BE the river instead of the whirlpool. You will still express an aspect of the river through your own little ripple, but you can be the whole river.

Nothing is more exciting or more wonderful because then you know who you are. You ARE the father, you ARE the mother, you are the Sun, you are the current, you are the Life that makes everything. You made this whole world! When you remember that because you have learned to obey your earthly parents and have consequently come to know your heavenly parents, then you can say what Jesus said, "I and the Father are one." The whirlpool and the river are one — the mother and child reunion. And you know that you are indeed a cell in the body of God, a finger on God's hand, a part of this wonderful being of light.

Chapter 10

A FAMILY OF GOD-BEINGS

People in a dream don't notice what is happening around them. Walking in their sleep they live in a world of imagination, a world of make-believe, a pretend world. The people of the Earth have been asleep. They have been in a dream. People need to remember why they came here and from where they came. They need to remember, not something that happened in the past, but something that is here right now.

Usually when we think of remembering something, we think of remembering something that happened in the past. A long time ago we used to see what was around us. We knew where we were, who we were, and what we were doing here. We have to remember to open our eyes and begin to see what's here right now. There is an aspect of the spirit of God, the spirit that we are all a part of, that is called the spirit of Truth. The Spirit of Truth calls all things to remembrance. The Spirit of Truth helps people remember things. How do we go about remembering things? Well, we have to stand back a bit from the things that occupy our thoughts and attention most of the time. Then perhaps we will begin to see a little more clearly.

Suppose you were a fly crawling around on a painting that was hanging on the wall. Suppose it was a painting of trees and ducks. You wouldn't really know what it was a painting of, would you? All you would see is a bunch of little dots. If you crawled around on one part of the picture you might see greenish-gray dots. If you crawled around on another part of the picture you'd see brown dots. You really wouldn't know what the picture was. You wouldn't know that it was a picture of trees and ducks. You would just see a bunch of little dots. You'd be too close to it. But if you moved away and stood back a bit, then you could see the whole picture.

All the things in our world, people, buildings, friends, schools, cars, trucks, these are like all the little dots on that picture. If our thoughts are usually taken up with, "What am I going to wear to school today? What am I going to do after school today? Which friends am I going to play with? I wonder what chores I'm going to have to do after school to day?" Then all we are doing is looking at the dots that make up the pictures of our lives. We won't know how to deal with those dots in a right way, unless we stand back once in a while and look at the larger picture that they are a part of.

It would be a good idea to stand back a bit from this world of ours and begin to look at the larger picture. Calling on the Spirit of Truth, we allow this Spirit to be right here with us. We let that magical Spirit move through our thoughts. We remember something that is happening to us right now. And part of remembering what is happening to us right now means that we have to remember why we came here, how we came here, and where we were born. Where was our beginning? Where do you think your roots begin? The roots of your physical body began in your mother, but where are your roots, your spiritual roots?

Did you know that you have roots in the center of the sun? We may have dressed ourselves up in these physical bodies, but we are much more than our physical bodies.

We are points of identity. Remember we talked about the one light and how it broke into many lights? Each one of us is a light, a spirit. The Sun that we see up in the sky is the physical body of a God-Being. That God-Being is a part of the One God that made all the stars in the sky. Another name for God is the Star Maker. One of the things that God does is make stars. These stars are physical focus points in the body of God. Stars are Suns when you are up close.

A long time ago we traveled from the center of this closest star. We didn't have bodies then like we have now. We had vibrational bodies. A family of us God-beings left the Sun in these bodies of light and traveled through space to create life on the Earth. We accomplish this by working as a sort of prism. The light from the Sun shines through this prism. The colors are reflected on the mirror of each God-being. Because of this the Earth is filled with people, people who were designed to reflect the loving nature of the Sun.

Each of these mirrors is different, some have tiny ripples in their surfaces, others are curved, slightly concave, or slightly convex. Some of them catch certain color rays as they are filtered through. Others reflect other rainbow colors. This creative energy lights up the people in the world. Human beings have bodies, minds and hearts that reflect the light of the Sun. If it weren't for the sunshine, all these little mirrors, all these people, wouldn't be alive. If it weren't for the spirit that lives in the Sun, we wouldn't have any light.

Have you ever seen a solor calculator? It doesn't have any batteries. You can use it forever. This clever little machine comes alive when light hits it. If we close it up and put it in our pocket, it's not alive because there's no light to make it come alive. In the dark it doesn't have any life. The piece of machinery all by itself is dead, it's not alive. When the light touches it, it comes to life. It's kind of like that with people.

As soon as the light from the Sun's spirit touches these bodies, minds and hearts, which are systems of circuitry like a calculator, we come alive. We have life. Where does life come from? That life comes from God. Our life is God's life. We each reflect slightly different aspects of the light of truth that comes from the center of being. It is the nature of being to share. Being really likes to share. God's spirit wants to share its life. God wants to have friends to play with. So God becomes many, many stars in the sky, each one a being of light.

Each of these stars in the sky has the nature of God; it too likes to share. So it allows its light to be divided through the prism of other God-beings into more God-beings, like the people here on Earth. Each one of us is like a prism that receives the light from God and shares it with the people in our world. We can remember our roots because they're not something that we left behind. They are still with us right now. If we love God, if we love life because it's so wonderful and exciting, then because of that love, we are connected up with the entire family of God-beings that have their roots in the center of the star we call Sun.

Love is like water flowing through rusty, clogged-up pipes. As love begins to flow through the rusty and clogged-up pipes, it begins to clear all the junk out of the way that keeps us from remembering. When we really begin to love, all the junk that is keeping us from remembering gets cleared out of the way. We begin to remember our roots, roots that go back to the very center of all being. This isn't something to believe is true. If you need to believe something, it's because you don't know it. There's a difference between believing something and knowing something. This is something that you can know for yourself. You can actually have the experience of knowing yourself as a part of the Star-maker.

When this happens you begin to see what's really going on. You begin to see yourself as part of a larger story — not merely as the little details that make up your world. There is a story happening here, a very interesting story. You are an important character in that story and the story isn't over. In fact, we're at the most exciting moment of the story right now.

Chapter 11

STARLIGHT, STARDUST

A long time ago, the people who were reflecting the light forgot all about the light. They got to thinking that they were something all by themselves. Imagine a solar calculator that thought it could figure out all kinds of fancy equations without any help from the light. People forgot about God, they forgot about being, they forgot about spirit. They began thinking that they could do whatever they wanted to do. They thought that they could turn their backs on the light. As long as people faced the light and kept the first great commandment, they had a lot of freedom. They could do all kinds of things. But when people began thinking that they could do whatever they wanted, they began to die. They lost the freedom to be what they were created to be. They didn't completely shut off the light right away, but they made it real dim so that just a wee bit of light trickled through. It wasn't enough to make them work properly — if you tried to run a solar calculator with a candle, it would act sluggish and tired. It would make mistakes. It wouldn't be trustworthy.

To have the freedom to be what they were created to be, people have to face the light, they have to face God. For thousands of years now people have been running around in a mixed-up way, slowly dying. There's no reason why these physical bodies and these minds and hearts, these little mirrors that are designed to reflect the spirit, couldn't live much longer. The oldest person that you know is probably only about 100 years old. That may seem like a long time, but it is really very short. People were designed to live much longer. Your body is made brand new every seven years. There's no reason why everytime it's made new it couldn't be made new perfectly. In Bible-times people lived to be 800 - 900 years old. Many people lived to be 300 and 400 years old. But as the centuries have gone by, more and more people have been turning away from the light. The more they turn away from the light, the shorter their time is in their physical bodies.

People have been like the fly crawling around on the painting seeing only a bunch of dots. They have forgotten the larger story. They have been making plans and doing things that are ruining the picture. The picture is the Earth. We could probably make a long list of all the things that are ruining the Earth. People are not going to be on this Earth much longer if they don't wake up.

God tried to wake people up several times. Jesus tried to explain, "Hey, turn and face the Sun!" He talked about the story that people are a part of and tried to wake them up. But people didn't listen, they didn't understand. So God began to talk to people from the inside, from inside their very selves, from inside their own hearts and their own minds. Little by little the light from behind the mirrors began gently doing things to help the people see from inside themselves that they needed to change something, that they needed to face the light once again. It is important that this happens. If it doesn't happen, a lot of people are going to have a rough time.

Do you know what God wants you to do? Just one thing: God wants you to be yourself. That's God's law: be yourself, don't copy anybody else. Don't look at other children, see what they are doing and pretend that you are like them. Be what you really are. Don't copy grown-ups either. Be true to your own nature. Be true to the design that you are made in. It would be silly if a calculator tried to be a typewriter. We can see how silly that would be. People think that by being something they aren't, they can have freedom. But they can't have freedom that way. Freedom only comes when we appreciate the magnificence of the design that we are and learn to function in that design.

No Our design connects us together. We are all part of God. God is growing something on Earth that can steer the Earth. There needs to be something to steer what happens on the Earth. There needs to be something to steer the plant life and the animal life and all the things that grow on the surface of this planet. The Earth is like a space ship sailing around the Sun. You know that on a ship there is a little rudder. The rudder steers the whole ship. You can have a huge ship, a tremendous ship, and it could be steered by a little rudder. But somebody has to turn the rudder.

God is the One who turns the rudder that steers the Earth. Human beings are supposed to be the rudder. God has tried to turn the rudder. He can see that the Earth is headed for a terrible trap. He grabs hold of that rudder and tries to turn it to steer the Earth away, but the rudder is made up of people and the people have turned away from God and are not allowing themselves to be a part of God. They're not being themselves, so they don't respond to God. And the Earth keeps getting in a bigger and bigger mess. We are a part of God's rudder. There is something that we need to do. We need to allow the love that we have for each other, for God and for Life, to connect us up again so that we can act as a part of God.

We can remember our purpose with God. We can allow the will of the Father to direct us. When we do, wonderful things will happen — things that can never happen as long as we are letting ourselves be controlled by what happens in the world around us, or by what we like and what we don't like.

If you had a model gasoline airplane that you could fly around by radio control, and you set it on the floor and let a baby play with it, the baby might try to drive it like a truck or maybe throw it and watch it fall to the ground. The airplane would be controlled by the wrong thing, wouldn't it? It wouldn't be controlled by someone who knew what it could do. The baby wouldn't have the slightest idea what the airplane could do. She might not even know that it was supposed to fly. If she saw a puddle, she might pretend it was a boat. It would probably be wrecked in a very short time because it was being controlled by someone who didn't know what it was for. People are in that fix right now. They are being controlled by something lower than themselves. Now if somebody came along who knew what that model airplane could do, she could make it do all kinds of wonderful, tremendous things. The baby would be surprised. Well, it's the same with people. We might be surprised when we find out what we can do when God controls us. It's as different from what people are doing now as a plane in a mud puddle is different from a plane flying around in the sky.

You don't remember these things in words, you remember in the way that you are. After you have acted in a new way — a way that is much easier — then you might be able to talk about it. But if you just sit there and try to remember, you won't remember anything because what there is to remember is something that we do, a way that we are.

The world that human beings have made is not going to be the same when you are older. The way things are done now is going to change completely. The way people go to

shopping centers, drive around in cars, and fly in air-
planes, is all going to change. The way people build their
houses, and the way they live, all is going to be quite different. These things will be different because something
basic is going to change: the way people think of themselves. Many people are already beginning to realize that
they are more than just separate and isolated people.
They are a part of a family of God-beings. They are a part
of the light that shines from God.

We can learn about the nature of our heavenly parents
by looking at their physical bodies. Our heavenly
Father's physical body is the Sun. Our heavenly Mother's
physical body is the Earth. Just as we know that we are
more than our outer physical body, so too the being who
has the Earth as her physical body, and the being who
has the Sun as his physical body are both much more
than what we see.

Everything that you see right now is made up of one of
two things, starlight or stardust. The only thing here is
starlight and stardust. It almost sounds like a fairy tale,
doesn't it? Well the truth is we are living in the most
wonderful fairy tale that anyone could ever imagine. But
because we wear the grave clothes, because we think the
heavy thoughts, we go around like a bunch of hypnotized
robots, thinking that things are serious, thinking there
are lots of problems, worrying about this and that, worrying about where the things we need are going to come
from. We should already know that everything comes
from the Sun. Everything comes from the being that the
Sun represents. And the Sun shines on and on and on!
The Sun shines forever! We can shine with the Sun
forever too, if we just learn to cooperate with the way it
all works.

The Earth here is stardust. It is star ash spinning
around and around the Sun, keeping warm. It hasn't

cooled off, the ashes are still warm. The light from the Sun shines on this Earth, our Mother, a symbol of the Truth. Isn't it wonderful; starlight shining on an Earth made of stardust! As the starlight shines on the stardust Earth, it burns a little. And do you know how it burns? It burns with trees, grasses, giraffes, lions, elephants, houses, bushes, fields, streams, rivers, and people. All life is fire in reality. Biological life is really a kind of fire, a kind of slow combustion. Each of us is a flame, a tiny golden flickering, part of the one light, part of the fire that burns on the Sun. And that Sunfire that burns in this nearest star has an idea, a good idea — our idea actually. It has decided to make people in its image and likeness so that we can shine like the Sunfather here on Earth.

END

It is time for people to wake up from the dream that they have been dreaming for thousands of years. It is time to wake up and remember where we came from, what we came here for. It's important to face the light, to do whatever we can to help our friends here remember their purpose and their destiny.

Why are you here?

Wouldn't it be a really different idea to consider; we chose to come here!

See Pg 96. the still small voice of God.

Chapter 12

TRACKING GOD IN AN ENCHANTED LAND

Did anyone ever tell you that you live in the middle of an enchanted country that has had a sleeping spell put on it? I hope you are feeling nice and awake. We're going to talk about the sleeping spell that rests over this Earth and how we might lift it, how we might wake up in a deep and exciting kind of way.

Part of what makes a spell a spell is the fact that the people who are under the spell can't see things that are right in front of their eyes. They only see certain things. The spell that is on the people of the Earth makes it hard for them to see some very important things, things that are right in front of them! Let's go on an adventure and see if we can uncover this mystery. Let's discover what it is that has been hidden from people. What is it that people have been unable to find?

One of the things that people have been unable to find is that magic which would solve all the problems that are on the Earth. That magic which would prevent suffering, which would keep people from going hungry. That missing something that would make it so people wouldn't need to go to war, that would make it so there wouldn't be people who cheated other people. That something that would ensure that there would be enough food. What magic would make this world an enjoyable, beautiful, exciting and wonderful place without sadness, misery and confusion?

Though people have looked for this missing something for thousands of years, they have never found it. But they have a name for it. They call it God. Everywhere people have looked for God, thinking that if they once found God, God could show them how they could make the world work so there wouldn't be troubles, so that people wouldn't have to suffer. And they're right — God could help solve these problems. God could make the world into a beautiful place again. But people have looked everywhere and have never found God.

Let's imagine that we're on an adventure. We're trying to track God. Now God must be pretty big, right? I'm sure His tracks look different from a rabbit's or a squirrel's. God must have pretty good-sized tracks. Somewhere in this enchanted land God has left some tracks. If we weren't under this spell we could see the tracks. We could follow the tracks and we would find God. Then God would show us the answers to all the problems that people have.

Now we know that the thing that people usually don't see when they are under a spell is the thing that is right in front of them, the thing that is right up next to their eyes. They are always looking far away. They are not looking close. What do you suppose one of the clues is that might lead us to God? One of the hints, one of the tracks that God has left — what do you suppose that might be? I think we could find it right now. People have been looking for this for thousands of years. What if on this very day we could find what people have been looking for — proof that God is around somewhere mighty close? There would be no question about it anymore. We'd know that we were just a few steps away from the One who made us. Maybe that's a clue! US!

Let's talk about your own body for a minute. Do you

realize that your body is more complicated than even the fanciest computer? And computers are incredible! A small desk computer has a memory that can contain as much information as a whole room filled with file cabinets, drawer after drawer filled with stacks and stacks of paper. All that information fits in a little computer that sits on the top of a desk. You just push a button and it comes up on a TV screen. Computers are the smartest thing that people have ever made. But let me tell you something: it would take a computer as tall as the Empire State Building filled with computer parts to do what every single human brain can do.

Your brain is the most marvelous instrument that has ever been made. People haven't the slightest idea how to make anything anywhere nearly as smart as a human brain. People have made some wonderful things but they haven't yet made even the tiniest bug. They haven't been able to make a single plant. People don't know how to make grass. Something as common as grass, even the smartest scientist can't make. People don't know how to make anything alive.

Our bodies are so complicated, you wouldn't believe it. If you could see the different systems that run through your body, you'd be amazed. Your nervous system is like a telephone network in a large city, wires going all over the place, here, there, everywhere. They all fit together in a precise way that transmits messages from fingers to brain, from brain to toes. Each organ in your body, your heart, your lungs, your liver, your kidneys, is like a small city. You even have your own postal service inside of you. You have your own telegraph service. You have your own television stations, your own television cameras. We have computers in these heads of ours that are millions of times smarter than anything that people have made. Now I want you to think about something.

Somebody must have made these bodies.

Somebody had to make this incredible instrument.

Remember we're still on our adventure. This is our first clue. There are other clues too. We look up in the sky and see the Sun, so big that many thousands of Earths could get swallowed up in it. And the Sun is just one of many stars in the sky. All those stars in the sky slowly circle around in their galaxy with planets that spin around them. There are billions of stars in a galaxy. Our Sun is just one star in one galaxy. Scientists say there are probably about four hundred billion galaxies. All that stuff is sailing around in the heavens, sailing around in the heavens perfectly, in perfect harmony, in perfect clockwork. Somebody did it! Somebody made all this stuff. There's got to be somebody mighty smart around here somewhere. These are some exciting tracks!

Now don't you think that the person who is smart enough to make these incredible computers that we drive around in, this person who made all the stars and galaxies and set them sailing around in the heavens so that they never bump into each other — don't you think this person is smart enough to fix things up here on Earth?

Well, of course He is. The reason He hasn't fixed things up is because people are supposed to help. We are God's secret agents. We've landed in this occupied territory, this land that is under a spell cast by the wicked witch of selfishness. We are undercover agents who have slipped into this enemy-occupied territory to represent God, to represent the person smart enough, and the only person smart enough, to fix this country up. How do we communicate? What kind of secret radios do we have? Do we have a little short-wave radio to communicate with God so that we can keep in touch, so that God can tell us what we need to know? Yes, each one of us does. I'm using mine right now. I'm tuning in to the God-being that made these bodies. He wants to tell us how we can hook up with His intelligence and bring that intelligence to the Earth.

Now we know that God lives in heaven. People have had a lot of ideas about what heaven was. People have thought that heaven was some place far away in the sky. Heaven is actually another channel that we can tune our radios to. Heaven is a vibrational level that is present right here in this room. In heaven God's will is done. In heaven God is in control and everything is perfect. On one channel, however, on this lowest frequency channel, people have allowed their machines to take over. People have let their computers make the decisions. That is part of how the spell has been cast. We need to hook ourselves up again with God in heaven.

God sends each of us what we might think of as a magnetic laser beam of light. This beam of light has a design present in it. When it shines on us, all the little atoms and molecules come up out of the Earth and they dance in the design that's inherent in the beam of light. God created us in His image and likeness. In every moment there is a beam of light shining from God. This is what will make us in God's image and likeness, if we don't let the wicked witch of selfishness trap us in her spell and block the light.

You know that a magnetic field surrounds each magnet. You can't see it, but you know that it's there. This magnetic field is like the light of God that comes out of heaven creating each angel — each one of us. We can see a magnetic field if we sprinkle iron filings around a magnet. The filings are drawn into the lines of magnetic force aren't they? The filings are drawn into a very specific pattern, a pattern inherent in the nature of the magnet. As long as the filings stay close to the magnetic field they're held in that pattern. They are healthy, awake, and they function in the design. But if they get too far away from the magnet, they get all scattered, random, meaningless, off by themselves. They are no longer part of a single thing. They are just a bunch of atoms scattered all over the place, just as people have been a bunch of lonely individuals scattered all over the Earth. This is also what happens to the atoms in people's bodies when people die. They go back into dust of the Earth. But as long as they are in the presence of that life force, sure enough, they center around the lines that are present in the invisible field of the angel.

Now this magnetic beam of light that God sends out for each of us contains our design. It contains the true pattern that allows us to be what we are, that allows us to be fully awake. If we go off to the side of that light, then we're in the darkness and we're not connected up with the intelligence of God that could direct and guide us and show us the right way to live. This light is a channel that we can tune in on.

There's nothing wrong with the vibrational level that we know as the physical Earth. There's nothing wrong with getting dressed up in physical bodies, minds and hearts. But we were designed to have an awareness of other channels too. While in this land, we are supposed to stay in touch with the vibrational channel where we are one with God.

Each of us is a ray of the Sun, a ray of the One God. We were never meant to lose our connection with our source at the center of wholeness. This connection is what people have been searching for for thousands of years. Reconnecting will provide an answer for all the world's problems. Any problem can be solved by simply changing the channels of your own being so that you are connected again with the source of all life and all intelligence, the source of the true design. You must allow the spell that has been cast on you by the wicked witch of selfishness to dissolve. It dissolves when you are thankful. It dissolves when you are grateful. Suddenly everything is made new.

Chapter 13

MIRRORS AND MAGIC

What caused people to lose contact with God and become locked into this lower vibrational channel? It was an event that we call the Fall. People fell when they startted being controlled by things that were in the subconscious realm. The subconscious realm has to do with sleeping. When you sleep you are controlled by what happens in the subconscious, you are controlled by your dreams. When you are awake, you know what's around you. When you are asleep important things might be happening all around you, yet you might not see them because you are distracted, distracted by all kinds of troubled dreams that aren't real at all. In such a state you are unable to see the clues, the signposts that can lead you out of this enchanted land.

Reality surrounds this illusion like the sea surrounds a fish. When we allow ourselves to be distracted by the things that are in our subconscious realm, we are controlled by something that we are supposed to have control over and we can't see the real world. We were created to have dominion over the Earth, to be the transformers, the radio stations that would receive God's word and speak God's word to creation. We are supposed to exercise a stewardship over this material world. Yet people run around like scared rabbits. If the weather is bad, then they feel bad. If there is a problem somewhere, they get scared. When somebody looks at them crosseyed, they get depressed. If their friends say a bad word about them, they get angry. People let every little thing that happens change them. They are controlled by all kinds of things that happen out there in the world around them. This is called the Fall. I'm going to tell you the story of how the Fall began.

There was once a boy who walked into a magic room. The walls of the room were covered with mirrors! His first impression was delight. He could see hundreds of reflections of himself going off in all directions in these mirrors — long, long rows of himself stretching on and on and on, for what seemed forever. He liked that. He thought that was neat. For a long time he played in this room with all the mirrors and had a good time making pleasant faces. He smiled, waved, made various movements, and watched all his different reflections make the movements with him. This boy liked to play with things. Because he knew that light traveled at a certain speed, he knew that some of his reflections could linger while he quickly ran over to another place and made other reflections. This boy was a creator. His name was Adam.

Adam shared the creative power of the God who made him. He was God's son. He played with these mirrors and made them do all kinds of wonderful things. He could cause certain reflections to play with other reflections. It was a wonderful and exciting adventure. But one day, accidentally, Adam made kind of a nasty face. He looked up and saw hundreds and thousand of reflections staring at him with this nasty face. He forgot that it was just his own reflection. He had been playing in this room for some time now, getting into make believe games with all these reflections. For the moment he forgot that that nasty face that he made by accident was just his reflection in the

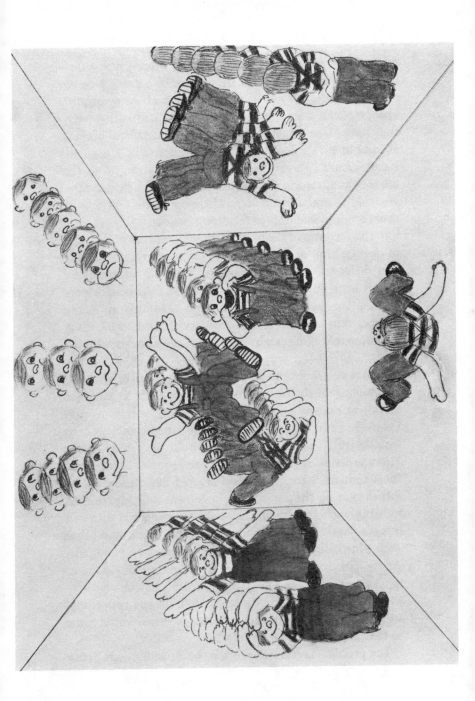

mirror. He grew afraid. He had never seen a nasty face before. He never even knew there could be a nasty face.

Can you guess what happened with he became afraid? His face got even nastier. Then he looked really ugly. Suddenly there were thousands of ugly reflections staring at him out of these mirrors all around the room. Adam didn't like all these reflections. He ran up to the mirrors and tried to change the reflections in the mirrors. He tried to grab hold of some of these images and change them around, make them different. Suddenly it seemed to him that crowds of people were coming at him and trying to change him, grabbing hold of him and trying to make him different. He started being different. Some of the people were pulling one way and some of the people were pulling the other way. This room was full of magic mirrors remember, not just ordinary flat mirrors. Adam got more and more frightened and more and more mixed up.

This is a parable about human history. This is what the true history of the Earth has been. People are looking out at the world and they are seeing lots of things wrong. People have made enough nuclear bombs for example, to set the Earth on fire so that it would burn like a Sun. There are alot of things that we can see in the world out there that are wrong. The Fall is what happens when we forget that all that is just our own reflection. Instead of fighting with the mirrors, instead of grappling with the images that he himself had created, all Adam had to do was, what? Right, all he had to do was make a good face. All he had to do was sit down in the middle of the floor, trust that everything would be all right, like the Beatles say, and smile. If he had just smiled, all the reflections would have smiled. A beautiful state of peace would come to that magic roomful of mirrors.

The problems on Earth are here because they are being

reflected by ordinary people like you and me. Few people believe that they can sit down and smile and everything will change and be right again. Can you hear what God is saying on the radio station on which he speaks to us? Can you hear God on the vibrational level where God exists whole and perfect? Can you receive the message that begins to trickle through?

The message begins to trickle through because a few people have tuned their receiver sets to this other channel. This is how heaven begins to be known on Earth. It is already present, just like all the frequencies that make up the various television channels are already present. Jesus taught that the Kingdom of Heaven is at hand, right here, right now. But we have to tune ourselves to it. We have to listen to it. People have not believed that. People have always thought, "Well, what good will it do if I change? Everybody else is the same way. The other kids are going to be the same way. The other people are going to keep being nasty. What good will it do if I smile? What good will it do if I am nice? What good will it do if I'm generous, charitable or friendly?" Well let's try it and find out! Let's give it a chance.

In the magic room full of mirrors some of the images that Adam created lingered longer than others. They didn't all disappear the minute he sat down and smiled. They faded out. Sometimes when you turn a light off in a room, you can watch it fade slowly for what seems like a long time. There will be a tiny glow there for a bit and then it will fade out. The false images and ugly faces in the room full of mirrors don't necessarily disappear the minute Adam sits down and smiles. And all the ugly things that are in the world around us don't disappear the moment that we start being nice and friendly. They do, however, begin to change.

When we put out positive, happy energy, those ugly

images in the mirror begin to turn into nice people. Some of the dragons turn into wonderful pets. Some of the monsters turn out to be really neat animals that we can have adventures with. A few of the nasty wizards and witches turn out to be our friends. It's good that everything doesn't change all at once. If everything changed instantly, what would happen to those people? They would all die and the little boy would be left alone. Adam likes those images that appear in the mirror. He likes to see reflections of various aspects of himself. He just wants them to be friendly, that's all — and he has forgotten how he can change them. He doesn't want them all to die. He doesn't want them all to disappear the instant he gets some of those images to sit down and smile. They are fun to play with. We can begin to experiment with this and see if it really works.

We can begin to walk along the road that leads to heaven. It leads to heaven by letting God's will be done on Earth as it is in heaven. As we walk this road we forgive some of the nasty images that seem to have done bad things to us. We begin to love. We begin to let God's love flow through us so that everything can be healed. We remember always that what we express comes right back to us. The face that we make is the face that we see. The face that we offer to others is the face that others offer to us. Jesus taught, "Do unto others as you would have others do unto you." However you treat people is exactly how you will get treated. If we begin to treat people in a nice, friendly, cheerful way, if we begin to really love people, this whole holy world will begin to reflect that love in a very short period of time.

If just one real person did like the boy in the roomful of mirrors could have done and relaxed and trusted God and smiled and was friendly and began to love consistently, within one generation this world would be healed and whole again. If two people began spreading good cheer and friendliness, it wouldn't even take a generation for this whole world to become the perfect paradise that it was meant to be. We can all represent the aspect of Adam that has already sat down and smiled. Vibrationally it's already done.

Something very significant has happened here on Earth in the last few years. Because of it something has shifted vibrationally in heaven. The boy in the mirrored room has already changed. It is now only a question of how quickly the rest of the images in the mirrors will begin to reflect the light and laughter of the new Adam.

As we allow the new heaven to be reflected in our every moment, we watch out for the ghosts that are drifting around from the past. There are some evil spirits floating around. Evil spirits that the boy generated when he forgot to have a good expression. During the time when human beings have acted selfishly, there have been ghosts generated by their behavior. These ghosts are drifting around in the world right now. They're real ghosts. Some people can even see them. They are like those lights fading out when the switch has been turned off. The switch has been turned off. These ghosts don't have any life, they don't have any power except the power that people give them.

These ghosts relate to specific bad feelings. Let's say that one of the ghosts is boredom. It's a ghost that drifts over a person and makes that person think, "Oh, this is a drag. I'm not interested in this." That's never really true. No matter what we're doing, that is never true. That is a lie. Anybody who feels that is believing a lie. No matter where we are, we are in the presence of God, we are in the present moment. There is always something unbelievably exciting taking place in the present moment. If one of these evil spirits comes and says "Oh, this is a drag. This is boring. I wish I was doing something exciting," we have to recognize that evil spirit as something that we need to deal with very firmly. We need to say, "Hey, get thee hence Satan. Disappear. Go!" We need to run that evil spirit off. Do you know what it's doing? It's depriving us of our life. Then we become lost in the tangles and briars of concepts and beliefs and ugly feelings. We are in the darkness, cut off from the light that shines from the eternal source of being. We can't let that happen. We allow the spirit of God to work through us instead.

Another evil spirit is anger. "Oh I'm mad at so and so. So and so didn't play that game fair. So and so cheated, moved their queen into my back row and put me in checkmate and didn't say 'checkmate!' " If we feel anger or resentment for whatever reason, we are being taken over by an evil spirit, something out of the past, something ugly and cold, something that comes from the grave. Evil spirits are grave and serious, aren't they? They lead us to the grave. They take our attention off the present moment where life exists. You know how people say they shudder when they feel a ghost? We can rightly shudder when we feel these evil spirits.

There are many evil spirits that drift up from the ground, from the cold past. They try to draw people into distorted reflections so that the Earth continues to reflect that forgetfulness that we call the Fall. But we don't want the Earth to reflect that any longer. We want the Earth to be fresh, new, alive, reflecting the spirit of our love, the spirit of our springtime.

Did you ever look in a baby animal's eyes? Or a baby human's eyes? It's like looking deep, deep, deep, into a bottomless well. Sometimes you can see the stars in their eyes. Sometimes you can see galaxies spinning around deep, deep in their pupils. Every one of us has that con-

nection with God and with the universe. When we decide
to bring happiness and peace into other people's lives, we
begin to remember our connection again. We begin to enjoy the wonder of this adventure.

You are a secret agent, a representative of the Sun,
bringing the light of creative intelligence to the Earth.
Your presence dissolves the ugly shadows that have kept
people in the cold, damp darkness. You participate in the
rising of the Sun, in what has been called the "Second
Coming of Christ." You participate in the most exciting
invasion that has ever taken place in the history of any
land . . . the invasion of the material realms by the forces
of light. There is nothing more wonderful. There is no
greater adventure!

Chapter 14

CHILD SPIRIT

Have you ever noticed that children have more energy than adults? Why do you suppose that is? Adults eat enough! They ought to have plenty of energy. They shouldn't get tired faster than children. Of course, energy really doesn't have to do with what a person eats though many people think it does. Energy isn't something that you can use up. Energy is like a river that turns a whirlpool. It is always flowing. Energy has to do with something Jesus once said: "Whosoever shall not receive the Kingdom of God as a little child, he shall not enter therein."

Something sinister has been happening to each generation of children since the Fall. The children, as they grew older, have made their childself a prisoner inside. They have let an adult copycat person pretend they were them. There is a child spirit that receives the world differently than an adult, a child spirit that lives in the present moment where the energy is! All energy comes from the present moment. The Kingdom of Heaven is right now. The present moment is the presence of God. When God is present, the Kingdom of Heaven is present and so is infinite energy.

We know that we are all aspects of God and that the angel that each one of us is, is a part of God. The child born into the world is a part of God, receiving its life from

God in the present moment. What has been happening is that as children grow older, they get more and more distracted by thinking about things that happened yesterday and about things that are going to happen tomorrow. It's like a sickness that every generation of children has come down with. As they grow older, the children began thinking more and more about yesterday and tomorrow — mostly because they were copying the big people around them who were also thinking about yesterday and tomorrow. They stopped noticing what was right in front of them. They took themselves out of the present moment where the Kingdom of Heaven is. They were no longer receiving like little children. They began receiving like most adults — through a glass darkly, through a foggy mist. The past and future aren't clear, their colors run into one another. As people become preoccupied with the past and the future, slowly the child inside of them gets locked up.

There is a story in the Bible that talks about this. Joseph's brothers didn't like him, so they sold him into slavery in Egypt. The Egyptians made Joseph work hard, but because Joseph received like a little child, he had a very thankful attitude. Even though the Egyptians made him work as a slave, he was still happy. Then the king, Pharaoh, put him in jail. That made it even worse. But Joseph stayed cheerful and happy. The guards noticed that he was good at managing things. So they put him in charge. He managed things so well, pretty soon he was boss of everything in the jail. Everybody did exactly what he told them to do and things worked out really well in the jail while he was in charge.

This story is similar to what happens to the child in people. As they grow older children begin copying other children, who are copying other children, who are probably copying adults. They begin imitating instead of being themselves. Instead of letting the child spirit within them do what it really wants to do, they play all kinds of games, some of them not so much fun. They become pretend people. The child spirit gets sold into slavery. The child spirit still lives in the subconscious realm and still is in charge of everything — keeps the heart beating, keeps us breathing, makes our blood flow, digests our food, takes care of all that stuff. Don't you think that whoever takes care of all that stuff must be pretty smart?

Do you have any idea how to begin to digest your food? What if you had to keep your heart beating? Would you know how to do it? What if you had to know how to make the air come into your lungs, and you had to know how to make the blood pick up little molecules of oxygen and circulate throughout your body and then go back to your heart and get some more and keep doing it? What if you had to figure all that out? It would be really complicated. But somebody is doing all that. Here is another clue that shows us that God is around here somewhere. The aspect of God that you are is in charge of your subconscious realm, taking care of all the things inside of your body. That God being is really smart. But that God being, that child spirit, should be let out of jail and allowed into your conscious realm as well.

We have begun to see that as children grow older, they usually lock the child spirit up. Do you know why? Do you know where that starts? It starts because they believe a lie. It starts when children believe the lie — that they have to worry. This is the first lie. When a little child first begins to believe that he or she has to worry, that's when the child spirit starts getting locked up in prison. That is how the bars of the prison are built.

The bars that lock the child inside are built out of fear. Fear enters in and mixes up all their thoughts so that they can't think clearly anymore. They get more and more mixed up. They feel like they don't know what to do so they start copying. But it is all because they believe the lie that people have to worry. People don't have to worry! There is really nothing to worry about.

It seems like there are things to worry about in the world the way it is. Just about everyone you talk to is worried about something. Some children think it's cool to look worried. Have you ever noticed that? A lot of young people think that when they look worried it's a sign that they are grown up. But do you know what? It's impossible to worry if you are in the present moment. If your attention is in the present moment, if you appreciate what's around you, if you give thanks for everything, you'll forget all about worrying. What a beautiful day it is today! There is nothing to worry about now, we all know that. But at other times it might seem like there is something to worry about. If that ever happens, remember that there is nothing that can go wrong. Nothing can ever go wrong unless you want it to for some mixed-up reason. The only reason you would want it to for some mixed-up reason is because you had already started to worry.

There was a man named Job who realized one time that whatever he was afraid of would happen. "What I have feared has come upon me," he said. It happened to him because he was afraid of it — because he was worried about stuff. If he wasn't worried, nothing bad would have happened. Do you know that there is nothing bad that can happen to any of you? There really isn't <u>unless you get mixed up enough to start worrying</u>. If you worry, you make it happen! Your thoughts are creative. They make things happen.

So we are thankful for each other, for this beautiful day, for this place to be. We are thankful for the time to talk about these things so that we can understand them later when others around us are worried about things and we pick up their worried thoughts. We won't copy. When we are thankful, we actually help God to make things. That's what we came here to do. We came here to bless things and to help things grow. When we are thankful we do that. When we worry, we make whatever we worry about happen.

Whenever anything seems bad, whenever you feel uncomfortable, or there is a problem that is hassling you, it is always because you are thinking about stuff that has already happened or stuff that is going to happen. Did you ever think of it like that before? Whenever you are having trouble, it is always because you are thinking about something that happened already or something that is going to happen. Grownups are really into this. Have you ever noticed what grownups talk about? Mostly they talk about stuff that already happened or stuff that is going to happen. Children usually talk about what is right in front of their noses. They talk about what they are doing. There are exceptions of course, but it is not a good idea to copy people. It's best to be yourself. Notice what is around you and give thanks.

Chapter 15

ELVES AND JUMPING MICE

There is an old Native American story about a mouse called "Jumping Mouse." Jumping Mouse used to run around with all the other mice as they did their little mousey things; nibbling on this, nibbling on that. It was kind of a drag, so every once in a while Jumping Mouse would jump up. He would get higher than the other mice so he could see farther. From up high he could see past the grubby little mousey affairs that the other mice were interested in. Once he saw a mountain in the distance. When he landed he told the other mice about it. They were sort of interested but mostly they were too busy with their mousey worries to pay much attention. So Jumping Mouse would jump up more and more often, and he would see more and more things. He would see past all the grubby little things that the mice were worrying about. The mice were always worrying about whether they were going to have enough to eat. They lived in a field where there was plenty to eat, but they were always worried about not having enough.

Another thing that the mice were worried about was that the eagle would fly down and eat them. Eagles do eat mice. Whenever they saw the eagle swooping down, they scurried to hide in their holes or hide in the bushes. One day something poked in one of Jumping Mouse's eyes and he couldn't see out of it anymore. Guess which eye he

lost. He lost the eye that he used to look at things that had already happened. He lost the part of himself that was always concerned with the past. Then a little while later he lost his other eye. What do you think that eye used to always be looking at? The future. He lost the eye that he used to look at things that were going to happen. Now he was right there in the present moment. He was no longer like the other mice, scurrying about, worrying about the future, thinking about the past.

Since Jumping Mouse had no eyes, when the eagle came swooping down Jumping Mouse didn't see him. Probably you know what happened next. The eagle ate Jumping Mouse right up. But then guess what happened! Jumping Mouse turned into the eagle! Suddenly Jumping Mouse was flying around in the sky! Remember he loved to jump up because he liked to see far? Imagine when he got to be the eagle! He got to be the eagle because he stopped worrying about the past and the future. Because he wasn't worried, the eagle caught him and ate him and because he was in the present moment, he turned into the eagle. How wonderful that was!

Believing a lie is the first thing that children do to cut off their energy. There are many lies that people believe. When they believe these lies, they are being controlled by the past. Things that aren't true are based on things that people think happened before. When they believe these things, they can't see what really is. They are afraid of the eagle. They can't see that the eagle is really their friend. When people believe things that aren't true they miss out on a lot of fun. They miss out on seeing a lot of neat things.

Once I saw something very special, but it quickly disappeared because I believed a lie. This is a true story. I saw some elves one time. I really and truly did. I was walking in the woods down by the spring. I'll never forget

the spot. They were as close as from here to that tree. All of a sudden I saw about a dozen little elves. They were about seven inches high, all dressed up in blue and red suits with pointed hats and little shoes on their feet. They were sitting on a branch. It was in the spring and the leaves hadn't come out yet. There were some dead leaves on the branch from last year and the elves were all sitting on this branch. I just happened to turn my head. I saw them just as clear as could be. Do you know what I did? I said, "I don't believe it!" And as soon as I said, "I don't believe it," they disappeared. They turned into brown leaves.

As soon as I said, "I don't believe it!" I realized that I blew it. You see, I was carrying around something in my consciousness from the past — I was believing a lie. I wanted to believe in elves but somewhere in me I didn't really think there was such a thing. So when I saw these elves, I said, "No way" and they said, "Okay" — poof! That was the only time that I have actually seen elves with my eyes. I've sensed them a number of times. I can often sense their presence and tell when they are near, but this was the only time I actually saw them. There are a lot of things like that. There are many wonderful, interesting things in the world that people can't see because they believe things that aren't true.

I've heard that some of you can see elves. I suspect you already know about a lot of this stuff that I am talking about. I don't want you to lose your ability to sense and see these other realms. People lose that ability by believing lies. When people begin to believe lies, it blocks energy. It sets up short circuits in their bodies that block the energy. Our bodies are like circuits. A circuit in a calculator is a bunch of wires that electricity runs through. A light bulb is a very simple circuit with just a couple of wires. Our bodies are circuits too. Energy flows through our bodies from God. This energy flows through two connecting points. One of the connecting points is the Earth and the other is the Sun. The Earth and the Sun are like the two poles on a battery. We're a circuit in between. We need to be connected.

When the poles on a battery are full of corrosion, they don't make a good connection. You can't start the car. You have to go out and unhook the cables and clean the poles and make the connections good again. In the same way, when we believe things that aren't true, we don't make a good connection. We have to clean up our act. When our lives are full of corrosion we don't have a clear connection with the Earth and we don't have a clear connection with the Sun. What is more important, we don't have a clear connection with Truth and Love that the Earth and the Sun represent. When these two aspects of God, Love and Truth, can't flow through us from the Earth and Sun, our bodies only get about half the juice on which they are supposed to run. As people believe more and more stuff that isn't true, less and less energy flows through them.

The older people get, the more they usually believe. Adults believe all kinds of things. They have opinions and ideas about everything. Children are usually more open to receive God's energy in the present moment. This energy is what lights up a child. God's energy is the child's light. If the energy slows down because of lies and worrying about things, then the child light becomes a prisoner. By the time most people are in their twenties, they've lost contact with their childselves. When they think about their childselves at all, it seems like it was somebody else.

This has happened to everybody since Adam and Eve first ate of the fruit of the Tree of Knowledge of Good and Evil, when the wicked witch of selfishness cast her spell on the people of this world. People die because they believe things that aren't true. As they copy more and more, the energy flows less and less. They get sicker and weaker and older. But do you know something really interesting? Usually, toward the end of their lives, when their body is only getting a trickle of energy, the copycat that took the place of the real child gets scared. He begins to see that all the lies that he believed in are actually killing the body that he was driving around. So he gets scared and runs away. Then, for a short time, just before many people die, their little childself comes back again. For a little while, their child spirit is back.

Usually though, it is too late by then because the body is sick. Blockages have caused the cells in the body to become hardened in patterns that correspond with the lies that they believed. The child is OK though. The child lives forever. But it doesn't have that body or mind to use anymore because it believed too many lies. This is a sad story of what has happened to people for a long, long time. I share this story with you so that you won't believe the lies, so that you won't let a copycat person into yourself, so that you will be yourself and do what your child spirit tells you is right.

There is never any need to worry about anything or anyone. You can trust your child spirit. Inside of us we know everything. God wouldn't have made us any differently. We know everything that we need to know for what we need to do now, in the present moment. If we are in the present, then we are connected with God. Since God knows everything and since we are a part of God, we know everything we need to know. It's really easy.

The energy that gets cut off when we believe a lie is the energy of Love. The lies have to do with worrying. And worrying is fear. Fear is what is there when love isn't allowed to be present. This is a good thing to remember —

worrying is fear, energy is love. If it ever seems that things are not going well, it is because you are not loving enough. You can always love more. There is always something to love. When you worry about stuff, that makes it happen. There is no need to worry about anything. Look at that Sun up there, always shining every day. There is so much love that floods this Earth, it covers everything. It surrounds us and enfolds us. God holds us always in the palm of His hand. We are so well taken care of. All we have to do is trust God. Isn't that neat? It's absolutely wonderful! Do you know what the best thing you can do for this world is? Have a good time. That is your fundamental responsibility. When you have a good time — a God time — a time characterized by the joyful qualities of spirit, you are helping to wash this world with the love and healing that it needs.

Chapter 16

THE HARVEST

ONE WORLD ENDS, ANOTHER BEGINS

The Earth is like a mirror. God looks into the Earth and the Earth is supposed to reflect the beauty of God, the strength of God, the joy of God, the peace of God, the love of God, the wonder of God, the excitement of God, the magic of God! It's supposed to reflect God so clearly that all the parts of God can enjoy each other, so that God can have friends. We are a way that God can share. But the Earth hasn't been reflecting God. The Earth has been like a dirty mirror, a mirror that is all smoked up and covered with smudges. Can you imagine looking at yourself in a filthy mirror all covered with smudges? You might see something blurry, something that sort of looked like you, but didn't look like you very clearly. This is what God sees when He looks into the Earth now.

God looks at a world that reflects Him in a blurry and mixed-up way. It's not clear at all. It's all mixed up. God wants the world to reflect Him sharp and clear like a clean mirror. People know that something is wrong in the world. They look at all the suffering, the mixed-up people, the mixed-up things that people say, the crazy things that people believe, and they want to make it right too. But most people just sit around looking at that dirty mirror arguing about what it is that is reflected there.

Some say, "Hey, look at that. That looks like it might be an arm." Somebody else says, "No, that's not an arm, that's a tree waving in the wind." Somebody else might say, "No, no, can't you see? That's a lizard." And somebody else says, "No, you are all wrong. That's not any of those things. Those are just clouds." Many of the so-called wise people of the Earth sit around and argue about what it is that's being reflected so poorly in the mirror. We watch people disagree with each other about what they think is being reflected. Few of them ever think to get a bucket of water and a sponge to wash the mirror off! Then they could see what's there.

There is a way that we can allow the mirror to be sparkling clean so that God's ideas can be reflected clearly in it. Do you know what some of God's ideas are? Us. People. We're some of God's ideas. When we are reflecting God clearly, we're clean. You know the feeling you have when you have just stepped out of the shower and put on some fresh clothes? Doesn't it feel good to be clean? It feels even better to have a clean heart. You are friends with everybody. You have been good, you have been fair, you have been nice to people. That is the kind of feeling that we have when we let the mirror be washed perfectly clean. How do we let it be washed clean?

We don't have to do anything. We just have to stop stirring up distortions by being so selfish. It's like steam on the bathroom mirror. As long as the shower is running, the mirror keeps getting steamed up. But as soon as you turn off the shower, especially if the fan is going, in just a couple of minutes the mirror is clean. We don't have to get out a rag and scrub the mirror clean. We have to stop stirring up all the smoke and steam that makes it so hard to see!

There is more to do here than just talk about these things. There is something for us to do. We're here to represent the spirit of God. We do that by being our-selves. When we are ourselves, we are friendly. We are friends with everyone. That is the best way that we can represent the spirit of God, by being friends. Be friends to the children at school. Be friends to the older people. Be friends to your parents. Be friends to everybody that you meet. This is doing the will of our Father who is in Heaven.

There is something else that needs to be present for the image of God to be reflected in the mirror — light. Even if the mirror is clean, if the room is dark, we can't see an image in the mirror. The light of God must be present. That means that there has to be some understanding of what this world is about. Each of us is an angel that has come on Earth and dressed itself in a body-costume. Each one of us is a being of light, an angel of the Lord, a spark from the fire of God.

We have existed and lived with God since the begin-ning of time. We will dwell with God and in God until the end of time. For this little while we are come on Earth to be His people so different parts of God can dress them-selves up in these forms and have a costume party!

Flames of fire might be able to talk to each other in a warm kind of way. They might be able to send smoke signals back and forth. But they sure couldn't have the kind of costume party that we can have here when the angels come forth. Angels are coming forth now. These next few decades will see the end of the humanly-created world. This is not the end of the Earth, not the end of the trees and the grasses and the flowers and the birds we hear singing in the trees. This is the end of the human nature world, the end of the world of heaviness, the end of the world of people who refuse to have a good time.

Jesus told of the bridegroom who invited guests to come to the celebration, to come to the feast and enjoy life. Many of those he invited were too busy. One of them had to take care of some cows that he had just bought, another had just gotten married, another one's father had just died and he had to go bury his father. They all had something to do. The people that the bridegroom invited to the celebration didn't come. Do you know why? They were worrying too much. They were filled with heavy thoughts. So the bridegroom said, "OK, if the people I invited won't come, I'll invite others." So he sent for his servants and said, "Go out into the streets, go into the shopping centers and invite everybody. Tell anybody that wants to come, to come. All they have to do is put on a wedding garment." By that he meant that if they were to come they had to have a good time. He didn't want them to bring a bunch of heavy troubles and woes into the moment. He wanted them to come with themselves in the here and now and to leave all their problems behind. The ones who insisted upon bringing their sob stories, who insisted upon telling everybody all about the terrible things that had happened to them and how they had been mistreated, had to stay outside. They couldn't come to the party. They couldn't come into the halls where there was feasting and merrymaking.

Many people put on the wedding garments and came in and had a good time. There were rules at the feast, just as there are rules now that we have to abide by as we wake up and realize that we are guests at a celebration to which God has called us. The rules are wonderful and easy . . . we have to trust each other, trust life, trust God, and love one another. Allow an easy spirit of joy to fill your heart and be a friend to those whom you meet. Share a spirit of welcome and joy with everyone.

Do you realize that troubles don't really exist? Did you know that? Sometimes it seems that people have troubles. But troubles don't really exist. There aren't any troubles when we trust God. If we really trust God we can release our concerns and God will take care of them. The first lie that people believed when they fell from grace was the lie that there was something to worry about. There is really nothing to worry about. Life is wonderful and light. If we worry about things, the things we worry about will buzz around us and buzz into our eyes and land on our skin just like a bunch of little bugs. They will pester us to death.

When we allow ourselves to be filled with a thankful spirit, when we focus on the things that are perfect and beautiful, then the few things that might not be just as we would like don't seem very important anymore. We forget all about them and they soon lose interest in us. The same is true with respect to our problems. They will lose interest in us if we forget about them. Insects are like this too, I've noticed. They are only interested in us to the extent that they can get us agitated and fidgety. When we get agitated, we dissipate energy, we spring a leak. The substance of life begins to run out and problems grow on that energy. We don't have to do this. We don't have to pay any attention to imaginary problems.

We can accept the invitation to be a part of God's celebration. We can put flowers in our hair. We can make bands of clover and wrap them around our foreheads. We can take it easy and feel good about ourselves and know that we are perfect beings created in the image and likeness of God. Yes, there are some things that we need to teach these bodies, minds and hearts. They haven't quite learned yet how to obey the angel that we are. But we don't need to worry about that; we can just let it happen. This is what it means to don garments of light. This is how we put on the bodies of light that God has given us. This is how we get dressed up for the celebration.

It becomes easier and easier as we go along because we

make more and more friends. Every friend that we make is one more love connection that brings the angel that we are a bit more out into the open. We do this for each other. We are friends to each other. We can be midwives in a way, assisting the birth of the angel so that that angel comes on Earth. Then the angel is born through our bodies, through our minds, and through our hearts. It is a birthday party too! We celebrate the birth of the wonderful angels that sing forever and ever and ever around the throne of God!

There are many songs that we sing. The song that we are singing today is the song of the physical plane, the song of matter. We sing this song on frequency levels that make it so that we can touch it, smell it, taste it, hear it and see it. That's how we sing the song this time. Today we sing the song of eternal being on the frequency levels of the Earth. We always sing songs of praise and thanksgiving around the throne of God. We have been doing this, my friends, forever and ever and ever — and we will continue to do this forever and ever and ever. But this song is a song that we haven't quite learned yet. That's why we talk about it; we practice our singing.

We practice how to sing in matter, how to inspire matter, how to sing songs that go right to the heart of the Earth, to inspire her to release her fullest potential in these human forms. We teach our forms to dance to the music of life, to the melodies and rhythms that proceed from the mouth of God. We live by every word that comes from the mouth of God. We live by every note that God sings as He expresses His eternal delight in trees, bushes, children, flowers, cows, rabbits, giraffes, elephants, squirrels and deer. We begin to see all of life as part of the song. We are chords and notes that blend together with all the other life-forms that are on Earth. Together we make some great dancing music. There is nothing more fun! There's nothing more exiciting! We're really just getting warmed up.

Are you beginning to learn the steps? We have to wake up before we can even hear the music. We need to tune to the channel on which heaven is evident so heaven can be made real on everyday Earth channels. When we are tuned to the channel on which God sings the eternal song of delight, we begin to let these bodies, minds and hearts sing with God so that all the Earth can share in His joy.

The day will come when all the Earth will sing with us a song of wonder and delight. In partnership with God, we will walk through the land and sing the songs that will go to the heart of every seed.

Each of you is a God-seed, sprouting to reveal the magnificence, the strength and the joy of the Lord. People are seeds of God. This is the season upon the Earth when these seeds are to be harvested. All those seeds that are growing in a healthy, cheerful, joyful way will be brought into harmony with the being of God. They shall awaken and remember the fruit that they are here to bring. First a seed sprouts, then it grows into a plant, then it produces fruit. The fruit only comes after it has grown for a while. So there is a fruit, a product, a love-offering that people are meant to bring forth in this season of the Lord. There is something to be harvested.

The seasons of growth can be as quick or as slow as we desire. The song of God causes seeds to rise up and express wonderful potential. The fullness of this cannot be known until there is a unified human family recognizing the fatherhood of God and the motherhood of Earth, honoring these eternal partners. That time can be today for us, though it may be tomorrow for much of our family.

God planted people as seeds, seeds that grow into castles, providing a home for God's awareness. Let's keep our castle clean so God can have a place to rest, so God can have a place to express. The Harvest is happening!

Chapter 17

THE LORD'S PRAYER

Did you ever count all the seeds on a wishing flower? There are lots and lots of them. And all the seeds — just think about this for a minute — all the seeds on a wishing flower came from one seed. When do you think the seed that grew all these seeds grew? It must have been last year. Where did it come from? It came from another wishing flower. First come the pretty yellow flowers. Then they turn into seeds and the seeds blow around and land on the ground and grow up into more pretty flowers which make more seeds. Where does it start? Does anybody know? Which came first, the seed or the wishing flower? If the seed came first, what made the first seed? And if the wishing flower came first, what grew the wishing flower? Wouldn't it have to come from a seed?

About 2,000 years ago on a day very much like today, a man names Jesus sat on a hillside with his friends and talked about many things. One of the things He talked about was the answer to the question: which came first, the mother or the child, the acorn or the oak?

Before seeds and before the plants that the seeds grow into, there is an idea in the mind of God. Both the acorn and the oak came into being at the same time. God had the idea for mother and child and created them both at the same time. First though was the idea. The idea was in what we call the heaven, the invisible world of God's mind. In heaven God's ideas are perfect.

✓ Jesus taught people how to pray. He said not to just say the same thing over and over again. He taught people that God, our Father, knows what we need before we ask Him. Our Father in heaven knows what we need much better than we do. We may pray for one certain thing, but God may know that there is something else that we need even more.

✓ When people asked Jesus, "How do we pray?" Jesus told them to begin by saying "Our Father." That's a nice way to think of God, isn't it? God is the Creator, a Father who cares about His children. He isn't interested in watching His children do things that are going to hurt them. God loves His children and if the children listen to God, God will suggest ways that they can be happy. So the first thing that Jesus suggested was that we think of God as we would think of a kind, loving father who really cares about us, who really loves us.

The Lord's Prayer is a way of putting into words something that our hearts already know. It begins, "Our Father which art in Heaven . . . " God, the One who created the whole world lives in heaven. In ancient times, people thought that heaven was up in the sky and that God, their father, was the Sun. This is partly true, of course, but we have to understand heaven in another way as well. Heaven is what is in back of everything that we see. Heaven is all around us. Heaven is like the radio waves that the radio turns into sound. Heaven exists on a higher frequency than the Earth. It is the realm where God's thoughts become the patterns and blueprints that cause the Earth-stuff to take the shapes that it does. For example, there is a thought of God (in heaven) that becomes an oak tree when it touches the Earth. There is another thought of God (in heaven) that becomes you when it touches the Earth. This is why God is the Father and the

Earth is the Mother. It takes both of them to make all the living things that we see: plants, animals, trees, birds.

"Our Father, which are in Heaven, Hallowed be Thy Name." Whenever we hear the word "name" in the Bible, it tells us something of the nature of a thing. The word "hallowed" is usually thought to mean "respected," but it actually comes from a root word that means "whole." "Hallowed be Thy Name" means "whole is Thy nature." Our Father who art in heaven has a whole, holy and sacred nature. His thoughts are whole thoughts. That is why He is creative. He is healthy, real and complete. His nature surrounds everything and gives life to all form.

"Thy kingdom come." What is a kingdom? A kingdom is a land that is ruled by a king. God is the king of the whole universe. "Thy kingdome come" means that we want God's ideas to come on Earth. We want His will to be done on Earth as it is in Heaven. We want the Earth to be the way God would like it to be. God does not want the world to be full of problems and troubles. God wants this to be a world where people are happy, where people share His life and joy.

When the Fall took place, people forgot that God is the King. They stopped paying attention to the laws that God had established to govern His kingdom on Earth. People stopped listening to the Word of God. Today people are no longer connected with God. They are no longer the way God created them to be. The Lord's Prayer is one of the most important messages that Jesus came on Earth to deliver. Jesus came on Earth to help break the spell that people have been living under for thousands of years.

In the Lord's Prayer Jesus said that we should forgive. Forgive anybody who does something to make us feel badly, anybody that does something that we think is unfair. These things are no big deal really. It reminds me of the story of girl's birthday party. This girl had just turned five years old. She was getting many presents. She had strawberry shortcake with candles on it. It was a tremendous day — all the strawberry shortcake that she could eat, plus one present after another. But do you know what that little girl did? One of her presents was a rubber ball. She had opened about half her presents and had eaten about half her strawberry shortcake when a little baby boy came and took the ball and started to play with it. She got all upset. Her mother said, "Oh, that's OK. Let the baby play with it now. You have other presents to open. You have your strawberry shortcake to eat. Just let him play with it and enjoy your party." But the selfish little girl threw a temper tantrum. Do you know what? She had a bad time for the rest of her party!

Here was a girl surrounded by all these great presents, her half-eaten strawberry shortcake still in front of her and she was having a bad time because a little boy was playing with her new rubber ball. It was so silly. It is hard to believe that it happened. But do you know what? When we don't forgive somebody, we do the same thing. We too are surrounded by tremendous presents. It would take us the rest of the day just to count the presents we have all around us here. Look at the beautiful trees. Feel the temperature of the air. Smell the clover. What great presents! It's wonderful how we have warm sunshine, or sparkling rains, or cold, crisp, snowy days!

We're surrounded with presents in every moment. We can spend our time being thankful for all those presents instead of getting hung up on some little thing that might not seem fair. Maybe things are fair, maybe they aren't fair. It doesn't make that much difference. In the central part of the Lord's Prayer, Jesus said that one of the most important things we need to do is forgive anybody or any circumstance that we might not feel good about. That makes it easy to be happy and light.

✓ What Jesus shared on the hills of Galilee long ago is still important to us today. It shows us a way to understand our world the way God understands it. The way God understands it is a lot more interesting than the way people understand it because it includes this whole realm of things called heaven.

✓ Scientists are just now beginning to discover the reality of this heaven that Jesus spoke of so long ago. Until a hundred years ago people didn't even know there were radio waves. They didn't know any such thing existed. When scientists first discovered radio waves and told people about them, people thought the scientists were just making it up. They didn't believe in radio waves because they couldn't see them. Today everybody knows they exist. There is an invisible world called "the heaven." Not everyone knows it exists yet. It surrounds everything that we see. Everything that we see in the material world, all the things that we touch, taste, look at, hear and smell, all these things are like receivers that pick up different frequencies, different channels that exist in the heaven.

✓ Today a number of us are beginning to feel, sense and talk about heaven. We are increasingly aware of a whole world that people have forgotten. We learn that heaven is what makes things happen in the Earth. If we're interested in helping right changes happen, it is important that we learn about this heaven that is behind everything, within everything, inside everything.

✓ "Thy will be done on Earth as it is in Heaven." Wouldn't it be nice if the Earth would reflect the Heaven that exists in God's thoughts? Wouldn't it be nice if God's plans could happen right here on Earth where we live?

No After the Fall people got lost in a dreaming, half-awake

state. They had wars, hunger, confusion, sorrow and despair. They were sad and mixed up. Thousands of years went by and some of the wise men began to talk about how things might be made right again. They talked about how they might wake up from the mixed-up, sleepy world. Most wise men imagined that what was supposed to happen to wake people up wouldn't occur until some distant point in the future. They would talk about heaven but they didn't know that heaven was all around them. They thought that if they figured out a whole bunch of complicated stuff, heaven might come again to the Earth. They used to dream of a Messiah coming — someone who would magically lift the spell somehow.

A few of the people remembered that there was a God somewhere. They were interested in finding out how God would make things right again. They thought that God would come back and, all by Himself, make everything right. This wasn't true of course, because the reason things went wrong in the first place was because people forgot the heaven. People were picking up the wrong channels. When God did come in the form of Jesus, He didn't talk like the other wise men about something happening in some distant time. The message that Jesus gave was, "The kingdom of heaven is at hand." The kingdom of heaven is right here, right now, all around. The kingdom of heaven is within, inside of us, inside of everything.

When we really begin to understand what that means, it is the most exciting, wonderful, joyous news! The kingdom of heaven is at hand! God is waking up here on Earth because people are becoming aware of heaven again. All the years of sleeping darkness are being lifted from the consciousness of human beings.

Heaven is something that we become sensitive to. We let ourselves listen to it. As we sense the kingdom of heaven, we sense God's presence right here with us. We listen to His thoughts in our minds and we act in a way that makes us a part of God. We begin to move with God so that we can help God make all the things in the world right again. This isn't something that God will do all by Himself. The reason the world is in a mess is because people have insisted upon paying attention to the wrong things. Today let's pay attention to the one thing that will make everything right and perfect and whole. Let's pay attention to the spirit of God and to the Prayer that Jesus taught. For His is the Kingdom, and the Power, and the Glory forever.

✓ Everything belongs to God. Everything that we see is here to magnify the glory of God. Wherever we are, we can celebrate the birth of eternal spirit into the Earth. In this moment we can allow Christ, the same Christ that was in Jesus, to be born into us. Jesus didn't say the Kingdom of Heaven was going to happen next week. "The Kingdom of Heaven is at hand" — right now!

Chapter 18

THE SHEPHERD'S PSALM

(Part One)

After the Empire of the Sun fell into the ocean, the people who had escaped began to habitate distant parts of the world. They went to China, they went to Africa, they went to Asia and Australia, and to the Mid-East. They went to North America, South America, India, Europe and out to the Scandinavian lands. They went to England and to Ireland. Some of them even went to Greenland.

Our story continues with a group of people who first went to the land of Egypt. As the centuries went by they moved out from Egypt, building settlements farther and farther away. One of the towns they built was called Babylon. In time it grew to be a great city. One day God spoke to a man by the name of Abraham who lived in Babylon. God told Abraham to leave Babylon and to go far, far away out into the country to a land that God would show him. Abraham did. He prospered in the new land.

After a while, Abraham had a grandson named Jacob. Jacob had twelve sons and each of these sons had many children and grandchildren. There came to be a group of people living in the land that today we call Israel. God called them the "Children of Israel" because they were all descendants of Jacob who had changed his name to

Israel. God wanted these people to be a special group of people who would learn how to be on good terms with God again and teach the rest of the people in the world what they needed to do to bring the lost Kingdom back to the Earth again.

In the land of Israel there was a king named David. When David was a boy his job was to tend sheep. He used to sit on the hillsides all day long — on days a lot like today. The winds would blow across the grasses and the sheep would gather around. His job was to make sure that they didn't go over the edge of the cliff, that they didn't wade out too deep into the pond and drown, that the wolves and coyotes didn't eat them, that they didn't get lost or wander away. So all day long David would watch the sheep.

Sometimes there was a lot to do. Sometimes he had to go running after sheep to get them back into the fold again. Sometimes a mother sheep would need help when its lamb was born and David would have to lend a hand. Sometimes there were sick little sheep that he would have to feed. Other times there were sheep that got stuck in the bushes or thickets and David would have to get them out. But quite often there wasn't a whole lot going on and David would just sit there on the hills and think about things.

David didn't remember the Empire of the Sun. Nearly everyone in those days had forgotten about it. Sometimes in the evening by the fire the old women would tell stories to the children about a time long ago when there was a land called the Garden of Eden where the people used to walk with God. David had heard such stories. But aside from these few fairy tales, he didn't know much about the Empire of the Sun.

David knew that there was a God somewhere and he could see that people were living in a bad and wicked way.

He knew that some changes had to happen so that the people would come back to God again. He used to imagine that God was a lot like a shepherd. And as he used to guide the sheep and keep them from getting hurt and lead them from one place where the grass was thinning, to another place where there was plenty of grass, he would think about how God would guide the people on the Earth and lead them to the best places if the people would only let Him.

When David grew older and became King, he used to write a kind of poem that is called a Psalm. One of these is called the Twenty-third Psalm. It is very beautiful — probably the most famous of all the Psalms. Let's all listen to it very closely. This Twenty-third Psalm contains instructions that tell people how to get back to God again. It is like a secret code that tells what people have to do to begin to see the Kingdom of God once more:

"The Lord is my shepherd; I shall not want

He maketh me to lie down in green pastures: he leadeth me beside the still waters.

He restoreth my soul: he leadeth me in the paths of righteousness for his name's sake.

Yea, though I walk through the valley of the shadow of death, I will fear no evil: for thou art with me; thy rod and thy staff they comfort me.

Thou preparest a table before me in the presence of mine enemies: thou anointest my head with oil; my cup runneth over.

Surely goodness and mercy shall follow me all the days of my life: and I will dwell in the house of the Lord forever."

In the old days school children were made to memorize this Psalm. Your grandparents and your great-grandparents, and your great-great-grandparents, when they were about seven or eight years old had to remember every word of this Psalm. It was something that their parents or Sunday School teachers felt was very important. Let's read through it together and think about what it means. It can show us the way back to an exciting and wonderful life again, not only for ourselves but for this whole world that we are a part of.

The Psalm begins, "The Lord is my shepherd." The Lord is God. Since God is our Father in Heaven, He knows what is best for His children. This verse, "The Lord is my shepherd" suggests that God is like a shepherd." What is a shepherd like? Let's think for a minute. What does a shepherd do? He guides the sheep, doesn't he? Sometimes he does this by himself. Oftentimes he has the help of a dog, a dog that runs around really fast, much faster than the shepherd could run and barks at the sheep, "Woof, woof, woof." When the sheep start to get too far out of the fold and start to go where they might fall over a cliff or break their leg in a hole, the dog comes running around beside them and goes, "Woof, woof." The sheep run away from the dog and run back to the fold again where they are safe and protected and where there is plenty of food to eat.

Have you ever thought that God might be a bit like this? Have there ever been things that went, "Woof, woof" in your life, suddenly changing something that you were doing so you began to do something else instead? I am sure that there were. These things are the hands of God. God had been called "The Good Shepherd." He is aware of us, always guiding us (if we let Him) to the best places. God always tries to bring us to the places where we will have exactly what we need. Sometimes we don't know what we need. Sometimes the silly sheep think they need to wander off into the desert where there is no grass. Sometimes silly people want to wander off chasing something that they think will give them pleasure or make them happy. But God, the Good Shepherd, knows better.

The next part of this verse is "I shall not want." "The Lord is my Shepherd. I shall not want." Did you know that wanting is the cause of all the troubles and suffering in the world? Everything that is wrong in the world is because of wanting. When children want something that they don't have, when they want to be someplace besides where they are, they separate themselves from the present moment. They no longer have their thoughts in a still happy place where they can reflect the reality of God, so their energy goes down. They don't have as much fun. They feel that they can't be happy until they get this thing that they want, whatever it is.

Often people go through their whole lives always wanting something else, forever chasing after something, and it always makes them sad. It often makes them mad. Have you ever wondered why people get mad — why there are fights? Because people don't get what they want. When people get mad and angry, they are not happy. They are like silly sheep wandering off in the desert. So sometimes when people behave in a foolish way, God, the Good Shepherd, sets up events in their lives that will guide them back on course again, that will bring them back to the green pastures. That's the next verse.

"He maketh me to lie down in green pastures." God knows what the right things are for us. "Green pastures" are what sheep like. What people like are the things that fulfill their purpose on Earth, the things that help them to become all that God created them to be. Separate from God, people don't know what they really want. We should listen carefully to this point and learn it well: people do not know what they really want as long as they are separated from God. After they become connected with God again, then God's will is their will and they can see what they really want. Right now the people in the world are cut off from God. They don't know what green pastures would be. They go chasing after all kinds of things — fancy cars, motorcycles, television sets, movies, parties, all kinds of things that they think are the things that they want. But God knows that they are not what they really want.

Have you ever seen a little baby playing outside who was hungry? Oftentimes the baby will start to eat stones and mud. The baby was hungry, right? So she started grabbing the things that she thought she wanted to fill her up. She would eat any old thing — rocks, mud, grass. Suppose you were that baby's good shepherd and you went over and you said, "No, no, no, your mother is inside heating up your lunch. Here let me take those pebbles out of your mouth." You reached into the baby's mouth and you started to take out the stones and the gravel and the baby got mad. The baby fussed because you were taking away what the baby thought it wanted. You were only trying to help the baby by taking all that dirt out of the baby's mouth so that it could be cleaned out to receive the food that was being prepared for it. But the baby didn't understand that, so the baby began to cry and fuss. It's a lot like that with people in the world. People don't know what they really want. They get to thinking that they want and need all kinds of things instead of appreciating what they have right now. God has already provided them with everything they really need. When people begin to appreciate what they already have, then God leads them beside the still waters. And that is the next verse.

"He leadeth me beside the still waters." You have probably seen how still waters, the still surface of the lake, can reflect the stars in the sky at night. When the waters are very, very still, you can even see the Milky Way. In the same way, the still waters of our hearts can reflect the magic of God. When our hearts are not filled up with desires, when we are not always wanting things that we don't have, our hearts become still. When we are not wanting things, or angry, or upset, our hearts reflect the magic of God.

When the magic of God is reflected, suddenly the Kingdom of Heaven is there for us to see! In any moment when we let our hearts be still, we can see the Kingdom of Heaven as it exists right here and right now. As we begin to see it, we can actually begin to live in it, to live our lives as if this whole mixed-up distorted world did not even exist. We can be a bridge from the sick world of selfishness to the healthy world of God's love. Then the soul of mankind, the spirit of people, can be healed. That's the next verse.

"He restoreth my soul." Restore means to heal. When our hearts become still, God begins to heal our soul. The moment we stop wanting, our hearts become still and God begins to heal our soul. Do you know what a soul is? When we look at each other we see bodies; we see legs, arms, head, torso. These bodies have different parts that we can see, but there are also some very important parts of our bodies that we can't see. The mind for example, is the part that thinks and talks; the heart, the part that loves and feels. The soul is the part that holds everything together. The soul is like a magnetic field that draws the particles into the pattern that reflects God, the pattern that is healthy. When we stop wanting, when we give thanks for what we have and when our hearts become still, then God restores our souls. We begin to reflect the reality of God.

Then what does God do? "He leadeth me in the paths of righteousness for His name's sake." The paths of righteousness are ways to use everything rightly. Righteousness means "right-useness" — the right use of things. People today have forgotten the right use of many things. There are herbs out here in the fields for example that can be used for all kinds of purposes that people have never discovered. Parts of certain trees here could be used for healing. There are many plants and mushrooms growing wild in the woods that people haven't discovered the right use of yet. But do you know what else we haven't discovered the right use of? We haven't discovered the right use of our own bodies. Would you believe that there are systems in our bodies that we don't even know about yet?

A little baby may crawl around for a year without knowing that it can walk. But suddenly one day another system kicks in and that baby realizes that it has the ability to stand up and walk. At first the baby may not even know that there is such a thing as talking. It hasn't discovered yet what its tongue or its vocal chords can do. It's got everything it needs to talk the minute it is born. But it is so busy wanting to drink milk and wanting to learn how to walk that it doesn't think about talking for a while.

When young people reach what we call puberty, around twelve or thirteen years old, certain glands begin to work. Suddenly a whole new system goes into operation. The younger children may know that the sex organs are there for a purpose. Maybe they have been taught this. They know that something is going to happen when they get to be twelve or thirteen years old. But when that system kicks in, when that system is activated, suddenly they are surprised. Suddenly they feel a lot different. Their bodies feel different. They start thinking about things that they had never thought about before. There is a whole new system that begins to operate. They didn't think about it much before then. Guess what? There are more systems. There are systems that people don't even know about yet, systems that won't begin to work until all the conditions are met that are listed in the first few verses of the Twenty-third Psalm. Not until we stop wanting and lie down in green pastures, and let God guide us where we need to go — not until our hearts are still, do we begin to learn the right use of all things.

Why do we learn the right use of all things? The Psalm says, "For His name's sake." For whose name's sake? For God's name's sake. The word "name" often refers to the nature of a thing. God teaches us the right use of our bodies so that His nature can be revealed. In God's nature, we begin to learn things that are as new and exciting as the awakening of sexuality, learning how to walk or talk. We begin to learn things that are quite different from what we have known as we have walked apart from God. God's nature begins to emerge through us. The reality of God is reflected in our lives. We reflect God's nature on Earth. God teaches us the right use of our minds then too. We begin to use our minds in a different way.

Have you ever tried very hard to think about something? Say you have a problem and you are trying to think of how you will solve the problem. So you concentrate very hard and try to figure out the answer. That's the way most people use their minds all the time. But right use of the mind isn't supposed to be difficult. Do you know how easy it is to breathe? It's easy to breathe; we don't even have to think about it. That's how easy thinking is when we just let the breath of life turn the contents of our minds. It's completely different from the way it was in the old state. It so much easier. It's much more refreshing and enjoyable.

The things that our minds begin to think about then are not the thoughts of fallen creatures who are separate from God; they are actually God's thoughts! What begins to happen (and this is so tremendous) is that <u>God thinks His thoughts through our minds</u>. And if you think that God doesn't have some exciting things going on in His consciousness, you're in for a wonderful surprise. God has some incredible plans, some wonderful ideas.

The right use of things often means that we find a balance. You remember the story of Goldilocks and the Three Bears. Goldilocks went into the three bears' house. First she tasted the porridge of the daddy bear and it was way too hot to eat. She tasted the porridge of the mommy bear and it was too cold. Then she tasted the porridge of the little baby bear and it was just right, so she ate it up — remember? There is a balance there. It has to be just right. The father bear's bed was too hard. The mother bear's bed was too soft, but the baby bear's bed was just right. Again there is a balance. There is a middle path, a central way. This is called the path of righteousness, the way to use all of God's things rightly. God will lead us down those paths if we trust Him.

Sometimes we might not recognize the paths of righteousness. We might think that things are right for us that are not. We might think that some seemingly exciting thing is right for us, but maybe it's not. Maybe it would make us sick. The sheep don't always know enough to stay in the herd. They wander off and the dog has to chase them back. Sometimes the shepherd of God's love is firm. Sometimes it's absolute. Sometimes it makes things happen to us that seem bad but they make us change our course. As we listen to the voice of God, He guides us. We don't have to wait for it. The voice of God is speaking in every moment. We just have to be quiet inside and let our hearts be still so we can hear. We remember patience.

THE SHEPHERD'S PSALM

(Part Two)

In the beginning you may not have understood all the things you read about here. Sometimes you understood a bit and sometimes you didn't. But as you are patient, you begin to get more and more interested. You begin to understand something. You begin to feel really good inside. You begin to feel calm. Maybe you don't know why but for some strange reason you just feel wonderful.

When we are glad to be where we are and who we are, tranquility is our experience. We feel the Lord's presence near. We feel Him everywhere around us. We sense Him in each other and in everything in our worlds. We feel His breath in the wind. We hear Him in all the sounds that come to our ears. Our Father lives in our hearts.

We know that we are not these physical bodies. We know that we are something more; that we are spirit and that we have physical bodies. We know that spirit is something much more wonderful than the bodies in which it gets dressed up. What kind of spirit is dressed up in the Sun? See that big yellow fiery ball up in the sky? That is the physical body of the local representative of our Father. It extends outwards to include our whole solar system. In the specific sense, the Sun is the body of our Father. Our Father is the spirit that lives in the Sun. Can you think of anything more wonderful? Wouldn't you like to get to know Him? Wouldn't you like to sit down and have a talk with Him sometime? Wouldn't you like to ask

Him a bunch of questions?

Our Father is an architect. He designed the whole universe. He designed that star up there. We're close to it so we call it the Sun. He designed the Sun and He designed all the stars in the sky. He designed the clusters of stars that we call galaxies. He designed the Earth and all the life on the Earth. He designed our bodies too. Our Father designed everything. But there has been a problem. The builders that were supposed to carry out God's plans have messed up. They rejected the most important stone, the stone of God's eternal awareness. The builders rejected that stone as they built on the physical surface of the Earth.

We are children of the great universal architect. We are here because we have a job to do. We're here to tell the builders that they had better start looking at the blueprint, that they had better begin to follow God's plans. People are on Earth to share in God's eternal awareness. The stone that the builders thought was worthless as they began to build on Earth was the most important stone of all. It is the state of consciousness that is to be the only state of consciousness once the Kingdom of Heaven is restored. On this channel of awareness there are many different beings and ways of looking at things, but they all share in God's eternal consciousness, the most important stone of all.

Let's listen carefully once again to the ancient words of this Twenty-third Psalm. People have remembered these words for thousands of years. There is good reason for it. These words are a secret key that can shatter the spell that has been cast upon the people of the Earth. Here's the 4th verse: "Yea though I walk through the valley of the shadow of death, I will fear no evil." The valley of the shadow of death sounds like a scary place, doesn't it? Do you know what the valley of the shadow of death is? It's the channel that most people on the Earth are tuned into right now. The Earth has been the valley of the shadow of death. Every generation of people that has come into this world has insisted upon doing the things that lead to death. All the children who have been born since Adam and Eve ate the fruit of the Tree of Knowledge of Good and Evil have grown quickly, withered like old prunes, and died. Do you think that is supposed to happen? Of course it isn't! Our Father, the great universal architect, has better ideas for us than to let us wither up like old prunes and die.

There is an important clue here in the word "shadow." What is the shadow of death? Let's think about that for a minute. There is a hint there. If the stone that the builders rejected is the consciousness of God, then the shadow of death must be the consciousness of people who are oriented in the Earth. The shadow of death is the thoughts that people think when they are busy worrying about what is going to happen in the future, or thinking about what happened before. When people are all wrapped up in thoughts of yesterday and tomorrow, they are casting the shadow of death before them. They will end up dying. The shadow of death always leads to the grave. Thoughts that are tied to the past and the future are grave and serious thoughts. They bring people down into the cold Earth until they are fit for nothing anymore except to be buried and to have six feet of dirt shoveled on top of them.

When people are always worried about the past and the future, they cast the shadow of death. People do this every day. Everywhere you go you will see people and hear people who are worried about yesterday and tomorrow. We can't let that turn us from the paths of righteousness. We understand the Twenty-third Psalm, so we allow God to guide us into green pastures. We have stopped wanting and we have learned the right use of things. Though we walk through the valley of the shadow of death, surrounded by people who are always casting shadows of death, we fear no evil, "For thou art with me, Thy rod and Thy staff, they shall comfort me." We know that God is with us everywhere. God is inside each of us, ready and waiting to shine forth from our eyes, to sparkle in our laughter, to dance in our minds and sing in our hearts. We know that God is with us. We fear no evil.

Nothing can hurt us unless we give our attention to it. The more we pay attention to bad things, the more they can hurt us. If we feel fear, it is a sign that we are doing something wrong. We had better wake up and pay attention. Usually the wrong thing that we are doing is resisting the evil, giving attention to the bad things. We'll never be able to help fix things up here on Earth if all we do is see the things that are wrong. We have to look beyond them.

We have to be so much in love with God, living every moment so fully, that we forget all about things that are wrong. Even if we feel uncomfortable at times, so what? Compared to the joyous song that God is singing in our hearts, it's a little thing! Even if we are surrounded by the valley of the shadow of death, even if everywhere we turn people are yelling at us and our things are breaking and we're stubbing our toes and things seem to be going wrong, so what? We fear no evil because we know that God is with us. We know that God sings joyous, wonderful, glorious music in our very souls. We listen to that. We give our attention to God. We worship the Lord our God with all that we are. We pay attention to the things that are right and true. Every day the Sun is up there shining even if you can't see it. Every day the birds sing. Even on cloudy, rainy days the birds sing.

Every day we wake up with a song in our hearts.

Every day there are things to be thankful for, things to feel wonderful about. We give attention to those things. We are thankful for what we already have. We do not want. Wanting things is a sickness worse than the measles, it's worse than the Whooping cough, it's worse than any cold you could every get. Do you know why it is a sickness to want things? Because when you have that sickness, it doesn't matter how much you get, you'll always want something more. It doesn't matter where you are, you will always want to be someplace else. It won't matter what you are doing, if you have that disease, you will always wish it was something else. Have you ever heard the story of King Midas?

King Midas loved gold. He collected all the gold he could get. He stole gold from everybody. He piled up tons and tons of gold. Pretty soon he had all the gold in the whole kingdom — every bit of it, piles and piles of it. And he still wasn't happy. It had taken him years to get it all. But he finally got every last bit of gold in the whole kingdom. Nobody had any gold left except him. Yet he was still sad and miserable. He had this wanting disease. He was never satisfied. So do you know what King Midas did? He made a wish. He wished that everything that he touched would turn into gold. The wish came true.

At first he had a good time. He touched the table and it turned into gold and he thought, "Oh boy, I can sell that for all kinds of money." He touched the chair and it turned into gold. He touched some books that were on the shelf and they turned into gold. For few minutes King Midas was happy. But then they brought him his lunch. As he grabbed his fork, it turned into gold. Before he had time to put the food into his mouth, the food turned to gold too. He went to drink his ale and as soon as the ale touched his lips, it turned into gold too. He tried to grab an apple, but it turned into gold before he could eat it.

Pretty soon he got awfully hungry. He couldn't eat a thing. Everything he touched turned into gold. A few days went by. Poor old King Midas was hungry and sad. He went to talk to his wife, the queen, and as he put his arm around her and started to tell her his problems, she turned into gold too! Everybody he shook hands with turned into gold. He couldn't even pet the cat.

So King Midas sat down and cried and cried and cried and he said, "God, I really am sorry. I don't care if I ever see any gold again. I just wish everything was the same as it was. I'll give you all my gold. I just want to be a plain ordinary person and have good food to eat and friends to be with. I don't care if I ever see gold again." Did you notice what King Midas was doing? He was wanting everything that he had before. God, of course, made everything all right again and Midas was a good king after that. He had learned a lesson. He lived happily the rest of his life because he never wanted anything again. He was content with what he had. And of course, it was always plenty.

"Thy rod and Thy staff shall comfort me." Sometimes a rod might be used to spank if a child was misbehaving, but how could that comfort you? Well suppose King Midas had a kindly godfather. Suppose when King Midas started doing all that foolish stuff with the gold, his godfather had whacked him a couple of times and told him to straighten out. King Midas might have avoided all the sad things that happened to him. He might have learned a lesson without needing to experience all that trouble. If we listen to God's authority and pay attention to the good shepherd's dog as it runs around and goes, "Woof, woof, woof" and tries to guide us away from things that might cause us trouble, we are comforted by God's firmness. Sometimes we don't understand why our parents say, "No, you can't do that. No, I'm sorry." But our parents represent the rod and the staff of God that can comfort us when we appreciate why they are there. Appreciating allows God to prepare a table before us.

"Thou preparest a table before me in the presence of my enemies." Imagine a circular table in front of us. The table has always been here but we can't see it until we do all the other things in these verses. Then we begin to see that God has prepared a table for us, a table with all the good things on it that we need, a table filled with all the things that are really going to nourish us and help us grow these bodies, minds and hearts into the image and likeness of God. This table is prepared in the presence of our enemies. We're not afraid of our enemies — these evil spirits that sometimes drift through the land, these ghosts that sometimes pop into our awareness and make us uncomfortable. We're not afraid because our Father is here! Don't you think that the spirit that lives in the middle of that Sun could lick the livin' daylights out of any little old ghost that might drift around and try to tell us to be sad? Don't you think that the spirit of the living God would know how to grab a bad spirit by the tail and swing him around three or four times and throw him off into the bushes?

When our Father is present, when we see the presence of God in our midst, we don't have to be afraid of our enemies. We can see the table right in the middle of our enemies. In other words (and this is an important point) things don't have to be right before we start enjoying life. We can enjoy life now, even though things may not always go as we think they should. There may be all kinds of things that we think aren't right. So what? These enemies don't mean a thing when our Father is present. He knows how to handle them and we are not fooled by the way things look. We're not fooled by the wrappers that might be put on ugly things.

Wherever God leads us is where we need to go. Do you know where God has led us? Right where we are. Every circumstance is a circumstance that God has created so that we can move in the direction we need to go. With everything that happens to us, God is working behind the scenes to make us move in a direction we need to go. He leads us to green pastures. He guides us over to the table He has prepared in the presence of our enemies.

"Thou anointest my head with oil . . . My cup runneth over." Oil is a symbol of love. As we sit at the table of life and enjoy the feast that God has prepared, He anoints our heads with His love. Our thoughts become thoughts of love and our hearts are still; they reflect the perfect love of God for His creation. We reflect love to everything. Our cups run over. Our bodies are like cups. If we keep trying to get our cup filled, if we go through life trying to get things to come to us, they run away. When we think that our cups are things that we have to fill up, they are never filled. But when we start wanting only what we have, suddenly we are full. Suddenly our cups run over and we have things to give away. We have more things than we know what to do with.

"Goodness and mercy shall follow me all the days of my life." You know why goodness and mercy follow you? Because your cup is running over with love. You are spreading light and laughter everywhere you go. You are making people happy, you are giving them something to be happy about. You are cheering them up. Whenever you walk into a room, people get happy. Goodness and mercy follow you because you have something to give people. You have the presence of God in your heart. You have the reality of life in your awareness. You can let that shine and let other people see it. This gives people hope in a world of darkness.

The very last verse of the Twenty-third Psalm is the

most beautiful verse of all: "I will dwell in the house of the Lord forever." You and I and all of God's children who want to join us, will live in the house of the Lord forever. The house of the Lord is our bodies. The house of the Lord is the Earth. The house of the Lord is all the stars in the sky. The house of the Lord is the Empire of the Sun. Because we love God so much, we don't have time for foolishness, we don't have time to think about anything else. We dwell in the house of the Lord forever.

Because we dwell in the house of the Lord, the house of the Lord begins to transform the Earth. People are healed. The places that we go are changed in wonderful ways. New things begin to happen. People begin to think thoughts that they haven't thought since they were little children. People begin to be happy again. Goodness and mercy follow behind us wherever we go. The Kingdom of Heaven enters this land of sadness and sorrow. The people who left the Empire of the Sun in that age long ago when our continent sank beneath the ocean waves, at long last, begin to come home again. They begin to come home to the presence of their Lord and King. They begin to know their Father, the great architect in Heaven. They begin to share His dreams and His adventures, His life and His love. His life is a million times more exciting than anything people have experienced since our home of long ago sank beneath the waves.

It is good to share these exciting days with you and to be a part of this wondrous adventure. How our story ends is up to you and me. Whenever things seem uncomfortable or strange, remember your eternal self and why you came here. Don't be fooled by the shadows. The valley of the shadow of death is just a passing fog being blown away by the warm winds of the rising Sun.

THE · END

Uni★Sun

We at Uni-Sun are happy and proud to have the chance to publish books that contribute to the New Age. Response to this author's first book, "The Starseed Transmissions", has been absolutely wonderful. Ken used the pen-name Raphael for that book since it was a totally "channelled" book — he had only to write down what was given to him. As we go to press with "Notes To My Children", Ken is nearly finished with a third book: "Terra Christa — The Global Spiritual Awakening". It should be available in the fall of 1984.

Should you be unable to obtain these books or any of our other products at your local bookstore, you may order directly from:

Uni-Sun
P.O. Box 25421
Kansas City, MO 64119

All of Ken Carey's books including Vision ($6.95 post-paid) can now be ordered directly from the above Starseed Seminar address.

(see prices and ordering information next page)